Make Money Teaching Online

Make Money Teaching Online

How to Land Your First Academic Job, Build Credibility, and Earn a Six-Figure Salary

DANIELLE BABB, PhD
JIM MIRABELLA, DBA

BICENTENNIAL
1807
WILEY
2007
BICENTENNIAL

John Wiley & Sons, Inc.

To my husband, Matt. He's the love of my life, has changed my world for-ever, and has shown me what a blessing it is to have the support of those you love. He is an inspiration to me in more ways than words can describe.

Dani

To Karen, my best friend and loving wife of 15 years, who has given me unending support with my profession, and to my beautiful son, Sean, who reminds me every day that I made the right choice. God bless them both!

Jim

Contents

Contents

Contents

Contents

Contents

Acknowledgments

To my co-author and dear friend, Jim; for his love of the profession and for believing in the integrity of our careers. And to his wife Karen for putting up with our project while we worked late and undoubtedly sacrificed family time.

To Bob Diforio, the most fantastic agent a person can ask for! He kept me in line, believed in us and gave us his best effort and expertise. I hope to meet you one day!

To Arlene, for her undying friendship, for love through good times and bad, and for always giving it to me straight.

To Alex for being one of my best friends, for keeping me motivated, for making me think beyond the obvious, for sharing a passion for life that not many do, and for "getting it." Thanks for making me laugh, even when it's at my expense!

Last but not least, to my family, who above all else always made me feel as though anything in the world was possible with enough hard work. Although I didn't become an astronaut, a judge, or any of my other childhood passions, their points made it across loud and clear.

Especially, to my grandfather, who is a never-ending supply of support and true loving inspiration.

Dani

Acknowledgments

To my co-author, Dani Babb, a great partner and valued friend. I was proud to be your mentor but I am prouder to be your colleague. Thanks for this great ride.

To Mike Bennett, my all-time favorite teacher, who made me want to be like him. You will never know how many lives you have touched and continue to touch as a teacher.

To Dick Murphy, a close friend and confidant, whose humorous approach to life is refreshing. Thanks for being a great sounding board.

To Julius Demps, my newest friend and mentee, whose attitude about education should be contagious. You are such an inspiration.

To Maria Puzziferro, a dear colleague, who gave us valuable material for our book from the administrator's perspective and helped make our book a tool for faculty and deans alike.

And to Cindy and Shane Stewart, our closest friends and my son's godparents, who are always there for us without fail. God bless you both.

Jim

Make Money Teaching Online

1

Introduction to Online Teaching

> *No trend has changed the face of higher education more than the shift away from a corps of full-time, tenure-track faculty to a contingent instructional workforce. That workforce includes part-time/adjunct faculty, full-time/non-tenure-track faculty, and graduate employees. Together these employees now make up an amazing 70 percent of the 1.3 million employee instructional workforce in higher education.*
>
> —U.S. Department of Education

Over 80 percent of learners today have taken at least one class online; this number is increasing and is expected to be nearly 100 percent in the next few years. To keep up with this heavy demand, most universities are turning to part-time faculty, in some cases for 100 percent of their faculty. This book takes you on a journey through understanding how and why online schools have been started, deciphering the good schools from the bad, obtaining jobs as online faculty, training for the faculty positions, retaining contracts, and managing courses. It will show you how to begin earning a living teaching online and then expand your work into full-time pay if you wish!

Our Experiences

Both of us are experienced part-time faculty, making a living at teaching online as what are often classified as *full-time part-timers*. We are well paid and very satisfied with our chosen profession. Every piece of advice we give you in this book is derived from personal knowledge, interviews with college deans, and/or research. We don't just talk or write about it; we both do it. Before we begin, we will introduce ourselves and share our experiences teaching online.

A Message from Dani

While working for a university for seven years as an information technology (IT) director and going to school during the day to earn a bachelor's degree, I decided to also pursue a master of business administration (MBA) in the evenings. Managing these three obligations was very challenging, but I decided the payoff would be worth it, and I was able to make it all work. Along the way, one of the department chairpersons for another school at the same university asked me to teach night classes on information technology for her program. I was intimidated and had limited public speaking experience, but I said yes and made a go of it. After that, the Blackboard online system was introduced to me as a tool by which I could teach an occasional class. I would be required to teach live (although Blackboard also supports otherwise), but online instead of in a classroom. I was immediately taken with the idea; it would help ease the stress of going into a classroom one or two nights per week in addition to my own courses, and I had moved quite far away from the school months earlier. Plus, my job was requiring more travel. By the time I finished my MBA about two years later, I was teaching a full load of courses while still serving as an IT director. I moved on to another IT job in a nearby city, but still taught night classes and online classes for the university for some time thereafter. I pushed more and more to hold my classes online because the commute to the university was easily two hours; after a long day of work, it was overwhelming.

After taking a hiatus from teaching for two years and focusing on my IT career, I decided to pursue a PhD—this time, entirely online. By this point I was tired of the endless downsizing, the shortsightedness of some Fortune 500 chief information officers (CIOs), and the frustration that went along with corporate America's lack of loyalty. The online degree I decided to pursue was through Capella University—it was extremely flexible, was fully accredited, and had an excellent reputation in the online world. It was one of very few online programs with doctorates.

I took classes for about 18 months at an extremely accelerated pace, since the average time to complete class work for a PhD is about seven years. I didn't have to sit in a classroom; I was able to stay at my office late (I was still working as an IT director for a Fortune 500 home builder at the time) and work well into the night reading, turning in assignments, and posting messages on discussion boards that I could read at midnight, at noon, on the road, in the United States, or out of the country. The flexibility I experienced as an online learner, as millions of others know, was incredible.

By the time I got to the dissertation process, I had heard from my entire committee, all faculty in my program, about how they were "sipping cocktails" by their pools in Florida while they were taking my calls and working, yet still providing incredible service, guidance, and advice. I finished my doctorate and within a couple of months had several teaching jobs online that were paying the same amount of money as my six-figure day job. I was able to handle both careers for a few months, but ultimately decided I'd give online teaching 100 percent of my effort and time, thus beginning my literal small business of one, me, an online teacher. I often work from exotic locations while traveling endlessly (and tirelessly) and have the life I always wanted. There are of course downsides to everything, but we will get to them later; they are minimal when compared to the incredible opportunities facing us.

I quickly realized that, as in any business, there is a strong list of do's and don'ts. There are ways to approach department chairs and university presidents with your resume, and there are ways not to. It's a steep learning curve, and can be a costly one. One of our goals in this book is to help eliminate those missteps for others and create a clearer, smoother path. I also learned that the online teaching community is very tightly knit and quite cozy, and most people you meet in the field work for institutions you also work for. Negativity about your work spreads like wildfire, but so do positive comments. Obviously the goal is to minimize the negative and maximize the positive.

Determining what you're best at, the particular value you add, and being the absolute best at it will ensure your success for a long time and will increase your salary considerably. I enjoy working with learners as their mentor, much as my mentor did, encouraging them to do their best and pursue their dreams. I have more opportunity to travel both within the United States and internationally now than I ever did as a senior manager in industry, and I enjoy the flexibility and academic freedom I used to envy in others with good teaching jobs. The difference is that I, along with other adjuncts, am an entrepreneur and I manage my online teaching as a business.

At first, many of my colleagues who also teach online were skeptical about a book that revealed many so-called secrets of teaching online; they wanted them kept secret, limiting competition. After many conversations with these colleagues, department chairs, deans, and friends, I decided that this new field offers a great opportunity that others need to be aware of, especially those juggling many responsibilities who still need a good income to take care of their financial obligations and/or families. The demand for online teachers is growing at a staggering rate, and existing faculty will survive the influx of new teachers. I became convinced that writing this book along with my former comprehensive and dissertation mentor, Dr. Jim Mirabella, was the best thing to do, and our respective schools have supported the endeavor. Our goal is to mentor you, assist you in finding online teaching positions at online universities, and help make being a teacher a sought-after job, as it should be! In turn we'll be helping the schools we love to work for by aiding them in their search for excellent candidates. What more can we ask for?

A Message from Jim

Back in high school, I idolized my math/statistics teacher, and wanted to be just like him. I majored in operations research and statistics in college and looked forward to being a teacher one day. After I graduated from the U.S. Air Force Academy, I was stationed in Alabama. I lived near Auburn University and asked one of the department chairs what it would take for me to come on board as an adjunct professor of statistics. He told me that he could use a good statistics professor, and if I got my MBA he would hire me. I enrolled at Auburn University immediately while serving as an Air Force officer; 18 months later I had earned my MBA, and true to his word, the department chair hired me to teach business statistics. I loved being in front of a classroom and couldn't get enough of it.

After leaving the Air Force, I sought out part-time teaching positions in the evening at whatever university was nearby, through several relocations. Eventually I found myself teaching an associate-, a bachelor's-, and a master's-level course all at the same time while working a full-time job. It may have seemed insane, but I was having fun, and I couldn't wait for my work day to end so my work night could begin. I was more concerned about building my teaching credentials than with growing in my full-time job, which gave me little satisfaction. I enrolled in a second master's program (in statistics) in order to enhance my academic credentials, but this required two nights per week as a student, so I had to juggle teaching with being a student, all while working 40 hours per week in corporate America. I really wanted to pursue a doctorate, but every program I investigated required that I quit my job and become a full-time student; as a married

5

man and primary breadwinner, this was not an option. One year into the master's program, I met with a recruiter for the doctorate program at Nova Southeastern University, who opened my eyes with an opportunity to earn my doctorate on the weekends without quitting my job. I jumped at the chance, and three years later I graduated.

Once I became Dr. Jim, my world changed dramatically. I was down-sized from my corporate job the same month I finished my degree, and immediately was hired by Florida Community College Jacksonville to serve as director of institutional research (a position that required a doctor-ate). Webster University, where I had been teaching for a few years, be-stowed on me the position of MBA chair, a position I have held since earning my doctorate. Jacksonville University, in applying to be accredited by the Association to Advance Collegiate Schools of Business (AACSB), cut back on its adjunct professors who did not have doctorates, so I was given more classes to teach. Then Webster University added an online component to its program, and I was chosen to be in the first group of professors; I learned the WebCT system and have been teaching in Web-ster's online MBA program for several years.

After 12 years' experience teaching in a classroom, my exposure to the online teaching world was at first uncomfortable, but after seeing it through I grew to love it. I realized that I could make the same money or more without having to work long nights away from home. I developed my own web site and began adding a Web component to my face-to-face classes. I searched the World Wide Web and applied at some online univer-sities, gaining experience in Blackboard and other Web teaching platforms. In 2002, when my job as an educational administrator became undesirable (100 hours a week without a pay increase, and no time for vacation), I made the bold decision to quit my job. I took a chance, knowing that I was already involved with five schools on a part-time basis and was earning about $40,000 yearly from part-time teaching. I asked the deans to give me more classes, which they did, and soon my teaching income matched my former full-time salary. I started applying at multiple online universities and received a lot of offers, but my biggest prize was an offer from Capella

University to teach in its PhD program. One year later, my income matched my highest annual income ever, and the following year my income nearly doubled. It was then that I began mentoring Dani toward her PhD as her dissertation chair.

Whether I am teaching in a classroom or online or I am at a doctoral colloquium, the single most common question I am asked is about how to make a living as an online professor. Students want my advice on getting hired as adjunct faculty, what schools are best to teach for, and what education they need to get. What we put in this book are the answers to many of the questions asked of us in the past couple of years. I have coached several people toward this profession, so I know my methods work. I also have a network of colleagues who are excellent teachers, and I have referred many of them to some great opportunities; this not only helps them, but it also ensures that I work with the best colleagues. As I have helped others, they have helped me.

I have also discovered the secret to job security: Teach a subject that is hard to fill (like statistics), teach it well, and teach at multiple universities. Having lived through a downsizing, I know the feeling of starting over, but now I am well positioned, and that kind of experience is a thing of the past.

Now I teach face-to-face classes 12 hours per week, and spend the rest of my time at home with my wife and son. I schedule my online teaching for when my son is asleep. I have even found the time to write three books, and I get to travel a lot. Now, with this book, I can help many others join this wonderful profession. Life doesn't get much better than this.

Substantial Opportunity Awaits

The world of online education is at our fingertips, and this means that many of us have an opportunity to work as full-time or part-time faculty members in an online capacity from the comfort of our homes—and earn the college credits needed to do that job in the same manner. Imagine:

More than 80 percent of individuals who are in a college program have taken at least one class online! Some of you already have a degree in hand and some teaching experience, some of you have a degree without teaching experience, and some of you lack both. Whatever the case, you need to know the market, what is required, and how to navigate the system before you jump in headfirst. This book will teach you how to prepare yourself for an online teaching career, where to look for jobs, how to get contracts, and how to keep them.

Can I Do This?

You may be familiar with online schools; you may even have heard of the big ones like the University of Phoenix or Laureate Education. The question you ask is, "Can I do this?" Yes, you can, if you have the motivation and determination! No matter what stage of your career you are in, there are opportunities waiting for you in the world of online teaching.

But I've Never Taught Online Before!

Have you heard the cliché "Everyone has to start somewhere"? The same holds true for online teaching. Every school you work for will require you to undergo a certain number of training hours and/or assignments. In short, the schools will train you! In fact, many even *pay* for training. Have you ever taught a group of people at work how to do something on their new computer system? Have you ever taught your children how to do their algebra problems? Have you taught your parents how to use their e-mail? Have you run brown-bag lunches at your place of employment to help everyone with a new training program or process? Most likely we've all taught someone at some point, and yes, this experience matters. It shows you can explain something clearly in a patient, empathetic, and detail-oriented way.

There are several online teaching systems that universities use, so even with online teaching experience you probably need some additional training for each new school you work for. Don't let this discourage you—you are also reading this book, which is a big step toward learning what to do to begin teaching online.

Who Can Teach?

To begin exploring this, we'll look a bit at who are making online teaching their careers. Many budding teachers are the individuals with doctorates or those who have master's degrees and are earning their doctorates. There are also former military personnel, full-time faculty members who are looking for additional income, corporate individuals who are degreed subject-matter experts wanting additional money and success, and degreed homemakers. Another huge pool is individuals who are retired but need additional income and have the experience and education to back up their new careers. There are even some with just a bachelor's degree who are looking to teach online in high schools. The opportunities are endless and the possibilities are great. We'll explore each one throughout the book, but will now review many of the possibilities in brief. You will quickly see how this relates to you.

Doctoral Degrees

The most coveted degree in academia is the doctorate. The doctorate is the highest degree you can earn, although you can further your education in a postdoctorate program or in another degree program altogether. The average doctoral degree takes longer to earn than a medical degree. The average time for completion by most estimates is seven years past the completion of the previous degree (although you can earn it much more quickly if you have the time and determination; each of us completed ours in less than three years). This is definitely a heavy undertaking, but well worth every effort. If you have a doctorate or are pursuing your doctorate, the opportunities you have available to you are endless and growing by the day. Your doctorate will give you an edge over other individuals who may be applying for the same academic position that you are, and may even give you an advantage in the corporate world. Your doctorate also paves the way for you to be able to teach at any level, from doctorate down to high school.

Master's Degrees

If you have a master's degree, you have plenty of opportunity for teaching. If you decide you want to make a career for yourself in academia, you should consider pursuing a doctorate, but you can still build a solid career with just a master's degree. You will be qualified to teach in some master's programs and nearly any bachelor's program. In the face-to-face classroom setting, only in community colleges or other colleges without graduate programs can an individual expect to advance without a doctorate; in on-line schools, the rules are quite different and you can make a very good living with only a master's degree.

Bachelor's Degrees

If you have a bachelor's degree and wish to pursue a master's degree, the opportunity to teach is a great justification to do so because a higher degree means more higher paying teaching positions with less competition. Some schools will even let you go from your bachelor's right to your doctorate, so check around. Although the opportunity to make a good living is not there, you can still earn supplemental income teaching online with a bachelor's degree. Look for associate-level programs online and certification programs for your particular area of expertise. For instance, some schools offer certificates in fields such as accounting or finance that don't lead to degrees. As such, they often don't require more than a bachelor's degree to teach in them. Professional experience counts here, so be sure to communicate it effectively. Also, read the section on online high schools in Chapter 4 to explore further teaching opportunities.

Former Military

Of the highly competent online professors we know, many, if not most, are former military personnel (including Jim Mirabella, former Air Force captain). We meet lots of former military in online education. Military experience is highly regarded in academia, and having this experience is often a bonus when looking for jobs. Having served in the military, you've already displayed honor, professionalism, courage, leadership, and no doubt incredible persistence. Who wouldn't want someone with those credentials on their team? You will still need a degree, but often the government will help with this. Use this advantage as much as possible; after all, you deserve the opportunity and have an incredible network within academia based on your military experience, even if you don't yet realize it.

Professionals

Professionals have a leg up in teaching online. In contrast to traditional education, where some professors have never left college, many online schools actually require that faculty have professional experience, not just a long list of degrees. Your professional experience will help you bring real-life examples to an online classroom, which is vitally important. You will see this exemplified in the section of Chapter 6 on resume writing and cover letters. Try to categorize your professional experience, then document it as well as you can; these are the areas you're most qualified to teach online, provided you have a degree. The combination of your education and professional experience can make you a valuable asset to a university because of the current emphasis on being a scholar-practitioner as opposed to strictly a scholar as in the old days. When you are an academically oriented scholar yet you also have experience in your field, this is highly valuable in that you can provide real-world knowledge to your learners and bring case studies and theories to life. You just need to know how to leverage your experience, because your experience counts more than you may think it does. In online teaching experience is often even required, which means your professional experience may be not only a leg up, but also an absolute must. Being a professional does not exclude you from teaching; some night colleges and adult learning programs actually require it.

Homemakers or Stay-at-Home Parents

Many homemakers or stay-at-home parents have left their careers for a while (or forever) to raise children. Many homemakers are also well-degreed, professional individuals who make outstanding online teachers. You can teach while your infants nap or while your school-age child is in class.

Retired Individuals

Many online teachers today are retired men and women who are done with their time in corporate America, yet don't want to leave the workforce. This may be due to their need for supplemental income, a challenge, or just a chance to give back to the community. The knowledge and experience that retired individuals bring, including professional experience and education, are highly sought-after in education. For example, in one of the schools Dani works for, about half of her colleagues are retired. They bring a wise view of the world, incredible experience usually from multiple organizations, and a broader vision on how things fit and why education is so important. Many tell stories of living near poverty until they worked their way to a master's or doctoral degree; what could be more motivating than to read notes from a professor with this type of insight? Retired folks are not dismissed in online education as they often are in corporate America; quite the contrary. They are respected for the tremendous wisdom, insight, and multiple experiences they bring to teaching.

Physically Disabled

Although a person can teach in front of a class while physically disabled, doing so does have its complications with regard to travel, as well as the logistics of lecturing and grading papers. The online teaching world puts handicapped people on an almost level playing field. Even if your handicap is speech-related (like stuttering) and would keep you from lecturing, it would not hinder your online teaching potential.

2

Online Schools: Are They for Real?

Teaching is not a lost art, but the regard for it is a lost tradition.
—Jacques Barzun

Many of us were told by our parents that the most important thing we could get was a college education. They told us to study, study, study, because the best schools would accept only the brightest students, and without a college education we would never go far. Just a couple of decades ago there was a limited number of colleges with a limited number of open slots, and most classes were held during the day when adults were working. What if you were an adult and hadn't yet completed or even begun your college education?

If you did not take this advice seriously, you probably found yourself with few options for an education beyond trade school and community college, as they have open enrollment policies without a limit on the number of students admitted. Those who decided to forgo a college education probably found themselves looking for ways to get a degree part-time while maintaining a full-time job and possibly raising a family. These personal and professional barriers often made it impossible to achieve educational goals.

Fast-forward to today and you will find that the Internet boom has taken the academic world by storm. As a result, there are countless opportunities to get a college degree without leaving home. Also, there is an entirely new career path for many: that of an online adjunct faculty member.

Many of you might be skeptical about this phenomenon known as online education. Is it for real? How rigorous are online schools? Can a person really learn this way? Can a person really teach this way? Is it accepted as valid and legitimate by corporate America? Would a college hire you to teach if you have an online graduate degree? Are these schools even accredited? What kinds of colleges are out there hiring online faculty? Aren't they just all a bunch of diploma mills? Why would anyone want to teach online? What kinds of faculty are they hiring? What's the catch? These are all valid questions, and you probably have many others. Let's take a look.

Is Online Education for Real?

Yes, online education *is* for real. In 1995, you might have been given a strange look if you told anyone about a degree you earned online. Most likely that strange look was one of doubt and suspicion that you merely bought a diploma! Now Internet courses are so common and so accessible that you can earn a recognized degree from a well-known university or college online, even if that school is across town, the nation, or the world. Internet access and ambition are the only requirements. There are many reasons for this trend: Online learning is on each individual's schedule, less travel time makes it more convenient, many programs are self-paced, and there is a wide variety of degree programs online to fit each individual's budget.

According to a 2005 Sloan Consortium report, "Growing by Degrees: Online Education in the United States," over 60 percent of schools offering face-to-face courses also offer online courses. Forty-three percent of schools with online programs offer degrees in business; 44 percent offer a master's program online. Over 50 percent of the academic leaders in higher education now see online education as a critical long-term strategy, with the largest supporters being institutions offering associate degrees. The online enrollment growth rate is more than 10 times that projected by the National Center for Education Statistics, and there has been about a 20 percent increase each year for the past three years.

Are Online Schools Less Rigorous?

As online teachers and experts on this subject, we are often asked by those we mentor and by potential teachers whether online degree programs are as rigorous as traditional programs. The answer? In many ways, they are *more rigorous* than programs at traditional schools. Why? Because accrediting bodies, which we'll get into later in more detail, didn't buy into online schools in the beginning. As a result, online schools had to work harder to achieve the same status as traditional schools. Some in academia don't like online education, and many Ivy League schools and those protecting their traditional ways don't agree that the programs are as rigorous. However, many of the founders of online schools came from traditional academia. Consequently, many online schools have traditional academics as their core faculty. Is there still some prejudice out there? Sure. But you won't care when you start teaching, earning a great living, and enjoying the well-deserved respect of your peers.

Can a Student Really Learn College-Level Material Online?

Yes, a person can really learn online. In fact, in many cases, a person can learn more efficiently online than in traditional classes. There are three different types of learning styles—visual, auditory, and kinesthetic. Visual learners, comprising 60 percent of the population, need to see the material to learn it, and they can accomplish this easily online. Online courses are by and large visual in nature, and learners are able to take their time with the material and read during days/hours that best suit their schedules and energy levels.

Auditory learners, comprising 30 percent of the population, need to hear the material to learn it. In a traditional classroom, they get this in abundance since lectures predominate in these classes; recently, Podcasting has been introduced, in which colleges put lectures that students would normally have attended in person on a web site for download to iPods. Online courses often have an audio component in which PowerPoint slides come with a recording or in which video clips show an instructor or outside expert speaking on the subject matter. This has allowed auditory learners who may have had difficulty learning online to take an online class with success.

Kinesthetic learners, comprising 10 percent of the population, need to actively learn, often by physically doing something. Whereas a visual learner can learn from watching a chemistry experiment and an auditory learner can learn from listening to the experiment being discussed, a kinesthetic learner must actually repeat the experiment to most efficiently learn from it. In online courses, technology has advanced to a point where a learner can actively participate in a lesson by using a mouse. There is software that even allows you to dissect a frog in simulation on your computer screen. In most online courses, students will solve problems or write out their thoughts and then submit them, making for an active environment that is, in many respects, tailor-made for a kinesthetic learner.

In a nutshell, students can definitely learn online—provided, of course, that they want to learn and are willing to do the work involved. Some students who tend to be shy in class or have issues speaking in front of others will prefer online environments because they can express themselves without feeling self-conscious. Additionally, those with serious time constraints can work during the day, take care of the family at night, and still find time for school because they are not being roped into a particular class schedule. As you might imagine, this often requires more self-discipline than traditional models, but with perseverance, online learning can be exceptionally rewarding and an incredible way to enhance one's career.

Can a Professor Really Teach This Way?

As we will attest, you can indeed teach online. However, the skills needed to be a good online teacher are not the same as those needed by classroom teachers. A traditional classroom will test your speaking and listening skills and your ability to manage short stints of time while engaging a class of students consistently. Online courses challenge you in a different way; they will test your writing skills, responsiveness, ability to manage a large number of students, use of technology, and day in, day out time management skills. Also, whereas traditional classrooms generally don't have prying eyes watching your courses and your work, often online courses are reviewed by individuals responsible for making sure you are doing your job since it's easy for them to log in and view a course. Both environments test your knowledge of the subject matter and your ability to assess students.

Some people are not cut out to teach in either environment, and some, like us, thrive in both environments. Students can hide in the back of a classroom, but they cannot hide online—you will know who is participating and who isn't. In large university on-site or on-ground classes, this may not be the case. Classroom discussions can often get out of control; however, you can easily maintain the control of an online discussion (although sometimes it is difficult to get the discussion started online if you have a bunch of students who just like to piggyback off each other's work). For instance, you might have a learner who copies sections of peers' work into his or her own post. Contrary to what you may believe if you have never tried online education, a teacher can truly get to know an online student, often better than a traditional student. You can more easily gauge study habits, work ethic, personality, attitude, and desire to earn a degree; you will learn if you pay attention to those you need to watch and what you need to watch them for! There are several strategies you can use when dealing with learners who are working unethically in the classroom: knowing each student's work, keeping copies of posts and documents to compare work, using a plagiarism tool, and typing text into Google to see if exact matches come up. Chances are the school you work for will have its own solution and will want you to follow its procedures. You can definitely teach online despite this nuance; after all, plagiarism isn't exactly a new concept. Whenever you run into an issue that makes you question whether you can truly teach this way, keep in mind that chances are someone else has already thought of a solution.

Sometimes you may question whether your work is effective. When former students tell you of their accomplishments thanks to what they learned from you, it becomes apparent that you can indeed teach online, and it is this regular feedback that keeps us wanting to come back for more. Such praise, and knowing you have made a difference in someone's life, is what should and does feed a teacher's soul.

Online Degree Legitimacy in Corporate America

Companies in corporate America that offer tuition reimbursement pay for accredited online education. Would any sound business pay for something that it didn't believe was legitimate? With over 80 percent of individuals throughout their college careers taking at least one class online, how can businesses not recognize online courses? There was a time when you might have felt uncomfortable applying for a job with your degree from the University of Phoenix, for example, but now you would be hard-pressed to find a large organization without a manager who has graduated from there or a similar degree program. Pressures to get a degree while maintaining job performance have essentially forced employees to consider alternatives, and online education has quickly become the most popular option for many. The incredible strength and growth of the Internet and the general acceptance of "online anything" in a global marketplace have only helped.

According to a survey conducted by GetEducated.com and reported by Vicky Phillips ("Are Online Degrees Really as Good as Their Campus Counterparts?"), the acceptance of distance degrees is rising sharply as Americans' trust in the Internet grows. In 2000, 79 percent of corporate managers rated a distance degree as good as a residential option, whereas fewer than 50 percent had held this opinion in 1989. This approval rating exceeds 90 percent when the name of the institution offering the degree is immediately recognizable to the prospective employer.

Can You Get Hired to Teach with Just an Online Degree?

Of course. With the number of online programs growing each year, opportunities for online faculty are growing, too. Schools have more demand than supply in many cases, so they are less concerned about university ranking than about accreditation. Trend data from the U.S. Department of Education available on its web site clearly indicates the move toward adjunct and part-time positions, with about half of all faculty positions being part-time. The growth in the online environment makes holding an online degree an even stronger position. There will always be some who will question your degree if it's anything short of Ivy League, but remember that there are hundreds of places that will hire you. According to the U.S. Department of Education, in 2003 there were about 540,000 part-time faculty members in the nation, and this number is even greater now due to the tremendous online boom since then, There is plenty to build your career on. If your heart's desire is to teach at a specific school, then be proactive and ask the dean what he or she looks for in prospective faculty.

Are All Online Schools Accredited?

No, not all online schools are accredited. We have made the decision not to work for unaccredited schools, but that doesn't mean you can't. We find it is one criterion that is important when reviewing schools to work for; we don't want to be affiliated with a nonaccredited school, and we have enough work to be choosy. In the beginning, you may have to work for one or two to get your resume built up and experience under your belt. The same rule applies when choosing where to go to school. The goal of accreditation is to ensure that education provided by institutions of higher education meets acceptable levels of quality.

There are many accrediting bodies that are not legitimate, but that allow a school to call itself accredited; the school must be *regionally* accredited for its accreditation to have any value. There are six regional accrediting bodies in the United States: the New England Association of Schools and Colleges (NEASC at www.neasc.org), the North Central Association of Schools and Colleges (NCA at www.ncaciche.org), the Middle States Association of Colleges and Schools (MSA at www.msache.org), the Southern Association of Colleges and Schools (SACS at www.sacs.org), the Western Association of Schools and Colleges (WASC at www.wascweb.org), and the Northwest Association of Schools and Colleges (NWCCU at www.cocnasc.org). These bodies list their accredited schools on their web sites. If you earn a degree from an online school that is regionally accredited by one of these associations, you can be assured that it will be as valid as a degree from any traditional university. Regional accreditation provides inherent validity that no other process or measure can, and it ensures that your credits are transferable. Most employers will automatically accept your degree, and if there is tuition assistance the program will qualify. Those schools that aren't accredited may be teaching the subjects well, but employers often will not help with tuition, graduate schools won't take your credits, and no respectable school will hire an adjunct with a nonaccredited degree.

The Distance Education and Training Council (DETC at www
.detc.org) offers legitimately accredited degrees. Through its own research,
though, it admits that DETC degrees are not accepted as widely as regionally accredited ones. The problem occurs when you want to take your
DETC degree and go for another degree. Many schools will not accept
your units as transfer credits.

You definitely want to earn your degree from a regionally accredited
college, then subsequently teach for one. Note that there are also forms of
accreditation that are tied to specific programs, such as that of the Association to Advance Collegiate Schools of Business (AACSB), and while they
are excellent to have, the regional accreditation is a core requirement first
and foremost.

What Kinds of Colleges Are Offering Online Courses?

Just a generation or two ago, the only types of universities in existence
were not-for-profit, traditional ones often remembered more for their
sports teams than their academics. You would find tenured professors who
were set in their ways and lifetime academics who believed that you
weren't learning anything if you used a computer to do it and who were
available only to students who happened to catch them in their offices
during their limited weekly office hours. Now there are four types of universities: (1) not-for-profit, traditional universities; (2) not-for-profit, nontraditional universities; (3) for-profit, nontraditional universities; and (4)
not-for-profit, bitraditional universities. The world is watching this industry intently, from the perspectives of students, teachers, and employers of
alumni.

Not-for-profit, traditional universities are still the most common educational institutions; you cannot watch a college football game without
seeing two of them in action. Many of these places are just now beginning
to enhance their classrooms with some distance learning, but many have

yet to offer courses that are 100 percent online, in part due to the resistance of their faculty. These universities are campus-bound, have tight entrance requirements, use traditional semester schedules (often 16 weeks long), and serve traditional students (ages 18 to 25). Some of these schools are now seeing their enrollments drop as students question their need to sit in a classroom. This was partly driven by the high-tech era in which many individuals got rich with an idea and a web site and decided school was best kept at a minimum while dreams were envisioned and goals were set and accomplished. Whatever the reason, the demand for online education is rising faster than that for traditional schooling. The only major exception to this is the typical college-age, college-bound high school senior, who follows the traditional path of going to a four-year college after high school.

Public university tuition is lower due to state funding, whereas private universities are expensive. You might also expect to see a teaching assistant delivering the lectures on many occasions, while the assigned professor is conducting research necessary to keep his or her position and to bring in grant money to the university. In this book, you will learn about the demand for adjuncts, who teach online most of the time; very few are core faculty who work full-time for the institution. As an adjunct, you might enjoy teaching for these traditional universities.

Most, if not all, of the nontraditional and bitraditional (i.e., a combination of traditional and nontraditional) universities are involved in online education, and some are 100 percent online. These institutions are where you can hope to build your career as an adjunct. They have many forms of delivery methods and semester length. Webster University, for example, has a traditional campus in St. Louis, Missouri, but offers courses at more than 100 sites throughout the world; at these sites, classes meet for nine-week semesters, one night per week for four hours. The traditional 36 contact hours is upheld but in fewer weeks than the traditional semester. Central Michigan University has sites throughout the United States; classes meet Friday evening and all day Saturday for three weekends, thereby also totaling 36 contact hours. Other nontraditional schools offer classes in an accelerated format, meeting for less than 36 contact hours; the University of Phoenix, for example, meets one night per week for five weeks. Still other nontraditional programs employ a hybrid format in which classes meet face-to-face for a specified number of contact hours, and online for the remaining hours. Purely online programs also fit into this nontraditional category, with semesters ranging from 5 to 16 weeks. Some online schools have a rigid schedule of weekly assignments; others, such as Northcentral University, allow students to work at their own pace, possibly completing a course in as little as two weeks. The point is that there are no set rules for these schools; contact hours have become less important since assignments are online and discussions and chats are viewed as adequate substitutes; and a three-credit course is more a function of the workload than of the hours of class time.

Diploma Mills and Scams

Many people ask us if online schools are just diploma mills (institutions that merely print out diplomas but fail to educate anyone). Unfortunately, some of the online schools truly are diploma mills. Some are not accredited, are completely unethical, and don't exactly make your resume sparkle. Others may even be regionally accredited, but they just take your money, make you endure courses with little substantive content, and give away inflated grades; those in academia know which schools these are by reputation. Accredited or not, diploma mills are the schools you don't really want to work for, be associated with, or receive a piece of paper from.

Many of you have received one of those e-mails offering you a PhD in two weeks—all you have to do is to send in $1,000. If you are foolish enough to send in your money, you will indeed receive a diploma in the mail from a legally created but nonaccredited school. You were sold a piece of paper, not an education. According to the same article cited earlier in GetEducated.com by Vicky Phillips, next to your home, education is often the biggest investment you will ever make. An education has become vital to the workforce, so companies selling bogus degrees have proliferated. David Linkletter of the Texas Higher Education Coordinating Board, an organization that regulates degree granting by private institutions in the state, says in the article "What's a Diploma Mill?": "Just to make people go through hoops of some sort doesn't mean they're going through the right hoops" (Bartlett and Smallwood, 2004).

College scams are closely tied, if not directly related, to diploma mills. Thomas Nixon, reporting on avoiding college degree scams in an article on the About web site (http://adulted.about.com), notes that we often see advertisements urging us to: "Earn a college degree in 28 days!" "Buy your high school diploma now!" "Get this prestigious unaccredited degree!" He says, "These are among the few advertisements that regularly cross my e-mail account touting easy ways to earn educational credentials quickly."

Nixon goes on to ask, "Would you trust a degree from Columbia State University? Sounds good, doesn't it? It did. Right up until the FBI raided it and the president ended up sitting in a federal prison. The degrees are worthless. Often these 'schools' will choose names that resemble real universities (as in this case, New York's Columbia University)." If this doesn't say it all, we don't know what does. As a teacher or a student, you do not want to be affiliated with these schools in any way whatsoever.

High school diploma mills are popping up as well. Since the mid-1990s when the World Wide Web took off at a consumer level, the number of these bad apples has grown dramatically. If you want to know your degree will be accepted by employers and academia, it absolutely must be from an accredited institution.

In an effort to avoid being caught as unaccredited, some diploma mills set up accreditation mills. Yes, you read that right. Before you go to work for a college, make sure its accrediting body is also legitimate. It is a sad but true tale of what we must deal with in today's marketplace. Many of these diploma mills take out expensive ads on popular Internet sites. Do not trust that advertisements are screened for legitimacy; this is not the case. The best of the online stores have made the same mistakes. Amazon and Google don't have the time or resources to check for such things. Unfortunately, as Nixon notes, many people believe that an advertisement on a trusted site must be legitimate.

Red Flags for Bad Eggs

One web site we use frequently, GetEducated.com (www.geteducated.com), lists 10 red flags that indicate a school might be a diploma mill:

1. Your chosen university is not accredited.
2. Your chosen university is accredited . . . but NOT by an agency recognized by the Council on Higher Education Accreditation, http://www.chea.org. The majority of Internet degree mills are "accredited." Problem is they are accredited by bogus agencies that they themselves have created. These bogus accrediting agencies often have prestigious sounding names.
3. Admission criteria consist entirely of possession of a valid Visa or MasterCard. Previous academic record, grade point average, and test scores are deemed irrelevant.
4. You are offered a college degree based on a "review" of your faxed resume. Credit for career experience is a valid option at many universities that deal with adult learners. But the process of evaluating career experience for college credit is complex. No valid distance learning university in the USA will award a graduate degree (Master's or Doctorate) based solely on a review of career experience. Undergraduate programs are more flexible. Accredited undergraduate programs typically limit credit for experience to a maximum of 10 courses or 30 semester credits. (One year of a four-year degree.)

5. You are promised a diploma within 30 days of application regardless of your status upon entry. Degree mills are in the business of selling paper. Ergo, they'll get that piece of paper to you as quickly as possible.

6. You are promised a degree in exchange for a lump sum—typically $2,000 for an undergraduate degree, $3,000 for a graduate degree. Universities do not commonly charge flat fees. They typically charge per credit or per course tuition and fees.

7. Your prospective online university has multiple complaints on file with the Better Business Bureau.

8. Your online "admission counselor" assures you that online universities can't be accredited by CHEA recognized agencies. This is a lie.

9. The school's web site either lists no faculty or lists faculty who have attended schools accredited by bogus agencies.

10. The university offers online degrees almost exclusively to United States citizens but is conveniently located in a foreign country, quite often a tiny nation that lacks any system of academic accreditation. Don't be fooled by online degree and diploma mills. Many maintain impressive web sites. All of them advertise heavily online. Look beyond flashy graphics for the name of the school's accreditation agency. Take the time to verify accreditation by an agency that is recognized by the Council on Higher Education Accreditation.

To date, according to Vicky Phillips, the CEO of GetEducated.com, there are more than 30 online diploma mills in the United States. Even if a school has real courses and a real faculty, without accreditation you will regret the time and money you invested. As an adjunct, you should stay away from nonaccredited schools, regardless of the salary offered. Even if they are legitimate, you wouldn't want to put them on your resume. Teach for them only if you absolutely need the extra cash, but remember that your experience there can be detrimental in the eyes of other schools, so keep it to yourself.

The controversy over diploma mills caused Congress to pass a law making schools ineligible for federal funding if more than half of their students or half of their courses are offered at a distance. The recent surge of purely online programs has caused Congress to rethink this law; an easing will undoubtedly result in an even greater growth of online offerings. Of course, this means that there is a chance for online diploma mills to grow, too, but it also dramatically increases the need for online teachers.

Now that you have a better understanding of who you're working for, let's talk about why.

Why Do People Teach Online?

People are inspired to teach online for many reasons: money, personal growth, the opportunity to give back to the community, as a stepping-stone to full-time employment, and so on. There are many different types of adjunct applicants, according to Dr. Maria Puzziferro, Director of Continuing Education at Colorado State University, Denver Campus. There are traditional teachers who have a wealth of instructional experience in the classroom but have limited online experience. There are moonlighters who seek to supplement their salaries and often have time limitations. There are administrators working at the college who want to earn extra income while broadening their horizons a bit beyond just knowing the culture of the school. There are recent graduates who are seeking their first faculty position. There are teachers looking for a full-time faculty position who need a foot in the door. There are retirees who seek part-time work only, and just want to share their knowledge. Then there are the full-time part-timers who, like us, are employed as adjuncts by several institutions, have a wealth of teaching experience, and possess strong technology skills (Schnitzer and Crosby, 2003).

Whatever your reasons for teaching online and whatever category of faculty applicant you fit into, we hope that you will get to teach what you love, and that you will love to teach. Doing a job that you love doesn't *feel* like a job.

So, What's the Catch?

Shari Wilson, who writes for *The Nomad Scholar*, discusses interesting perspectives about being an adjunct in her 2006 article "The Transient Academic." In the more traditional universities and community colleges that offer online programs, an adjunct is often considered an afterthought. No one counts on adjuncts to stick around, and adjuncts don't count on schools to keep them, but they continue to hope. Often given no training and no support, adjuncts may be tempted to water down the curriculum and deliver the most student-pleasing assignments, thereby assuring themselves of better evaluations while working less. Adjuncts often get bumped from their courses in favor of full-time faculty members whose classes have been cancelled, and are rarely invited to faculty functions. They are often just hired help without loyalty to an institution, and are rarely considered for full-time positions, although they might be promised to be in the running.

Rob Capriccioso, in his 2005 article "Help Wanted: Low-Cost Adjuncts," writes that there are growing opportunities for adjuncts to teach the equivalent of a full-time faculty load while earning adjunct salary. For 60 percent less pay and no health care benefits, pension, office space, or paid vacation, these hardworking adjuncts fill the duties of a full-time faculty member for much less than half the price. Students are essentially getting cheap labor for faculty in most of their classes while tuition continues to skyrocket. With these low-cost faculty even a small class can generate a profit for the college, and a standard-sized class is highly lucrative. Schools do not bluntly advertise this, but the message is clear.

To put the cost in perspective, a recently released College and University Personnel Association (CUPA) survey reveals that in a school of business, a full-time professor at a four-year institution earns an average of $102,000 per year and a nontenured professor earns an average of $49,000 per year (http://cupahr.org, 2006). Compare these professors to the adjunct who earns about $2,000 per course without benefits, and you can see how a school can improve its finances by hiring more adjuncts. Obviously, as online teachers we have to take on more work than traditional faculty does to make a fair wage, so there is undoubtedly a fairness issue at stake. Adjuncts can feel as though their jobs are at risk if they complain, and they just might be. Adjuncts, on the outside, seem to be overused and abused for far less money and hardly any respect. Without the protection of tenure, adjuncts must constantly prove themselves to get rehired. There is no consistency in adjuncts' paychecks, health insurance is self-funded, vacation days are really unpaid semesters off, there are many bosses to please, colleagues are barely acquaintances, and respect is hard to earn. Yet, as you'll see, there are many benefits that are difficult to quantify. We just mention these disadvantages because we want you to go into this profession with your eyes wide open.

The U.S. Department of Education posted the numbers in Table 2.1 for 2001 (note the heavy reliance on adjuncts, good for us if we want to continue working in this field!).

A 2005 article in *The Chronicle of Higher Education*, "More Faculty Jobs Go to Part-Timers," notes that new faculty jobs in higher education have gone disproportionately to adjuncts, with a surprising amount of hiring being done by the for-profit sector (these are often purely online schools that are sometimes even public companies). In 2003, the hiring increase for part-timers was 10 percent, while the increase for full-timers was only 2 percent.

The rise of online universities has given way to a new life for adjuncts where there is little or no tenured, full-time faculty—and therefore we are

Table 2.1 **Total Postsecondary Instructional Workforce, by Employment Type**

Category	Number	Percent of Total
Full-time, tenure/tenure-track faculty	405,805	30
Full-time, non-tenure-track faculty	198,787	15
Part-time/adjunct faculty	468,890	35
Graduate employees	259,567	20
Total	1,333,049	100

Source: U.S. Department of Education, National Center for Education Statistics, 2001 Fall Staff Survey.

it at many colleges. Instead of being the hired help at a local traditional university working for a pittance, an adjunct can work at limitless nontraditional universities around the globe for competitive wages. In some colleges, adjunct faculty have even begun to unionize in the hope of securing better pay and possibly health benefits, but these often come with a contractual agreement that means sacrificing some of the freedom of being an adjunct. Although adjuncts don't have the benefits of full-timers, they also don't have the same obligations for meetings, committees, ceremonies, and advisees.

Adjuncts may teach anywhere and everywhere. By contrast, full-timers are typically prohibited from teaching at other institutions, so their teaching pay is limited, while adjuncts have limitless potential (if they are willing to put in the effort and make the commitment). Adjuncts also keep up with the changing world of education, while full-timers tend to know only the world that they are in. While an adjunct may have to teach twice as much to match the pay of a full-timer, an adjunct may choose to teach four times as much and double a full-timer's wages without dealing with school politics.

There is no official job security in working as an adjunct that matches that of tenure; but, in a world where adjuncts are suddenly in the greatest demand, doing a good job and playing the game right can give you all the job security you need to build your future without fear.

3

Preparing Yourself for Teaching Opportunities

We teach what we like to learn and the reason many people go into teaching is vicariously to re-experience the primary joy experienced the first time they learned something they loved.

—Stephen Brookfield, Professor and Author

So you have decided to give online teaching a try. Congratulations! It's a rewarding career. If you have your graduate degree, you can begin to apply for teaching positions right away. If you don't have your graduate degree, you need to look for ways to get that degree quickly and in a way that fits your schedule while emphasizing your work in training others and teaching people. That doesn't mean you cannot teach without a graduate degree, but you would be limited mainly to online high schools; this would give you some experience while paying poorly (plus it is not the same to teach high school teenagers who are mandated to be in school versus adults who choose to be there). You might consider earning your degree online completely or partially since you will be teaching online. Whatever you decide, you need to start looking for schools at which to teach.

There are hundreds of legitimate, accredited colleges and universities in the United States where you can teach online with a master's degree. Some schools award only one or two specific degrees (e.g., business, psychology, education), but most offer a multitude of degrees. While the opportunities to teach with a doctorate are even greater due to the lack of qualified candidates (the greater your credentials the more doors will open), you can embark on this new career with a master's and do fine; however, we recommend that those who are serious about making this a full-time commitment pursue a doctorate at some point. A doctorate will substantially increase your income potential and get you through the door of most colleges. If you have only a bachelor's degree, though, don't despair; try focusing on your qualifications. Write them down if you need to, focusing specifically on your experience training others, your professional teaching experience if you have it, and your postbachelor's training. There are online high schools, some associate degree programs, and even some bachelor's degree programs that will let you teach for them, although you might have to work for some unaccredited schools. So from here, let's look at getting your master's degree, since the focus is on making a living by teaching online rather than just supplementing your income.

Getting Your Master's Degree

If you already have your master's degree, you're in good shape! If not, there are many excellent opportunities to earn one in about 18 months. Since it takes a few months to be hired at most schools anyway, you can start earning your master's, and when you get near completion then you can begin sending your resume out there. There is probably a university near you that offers a master's degree, most likely a master of business administration (MBA). Some of these local universities offer some or all of their courses online, too, so you could choose to take some courses face-to-face and others online (giving you much needed experience online from the learner perspective, a selling point even if your degree isn't completed yet).

For those concerned about earning a degree online, this is an excellent way to get the best of both worlds (i.e., you get to try out online courses in subjects where you are most comfortable).

You can also search the Web for the hundreds of online programs all over the world. Some are 100 percent online (e.g., Capella University and Walden University); others are from schools that also offer face-to-face classes (e.g., DeVry University and the University of Phoenix). Yet others are from schools with traditional degrees whose online courses are generally taught by the same faculty (e.g., Pennsylvania State University and Boston University). Bookstores, magazines, and the Internet can be sources of many excellent books on colleges. The 100 percent online and the nontraditional online schools can easily be found through a Google search, or you can visit one of the many informative web sites on the subject, such as:

info.theonlinedegree.com

www.adjunctnation.com

www.chronicle.com

www.degreeinfo.com

www.educationcenteronline.org

www.elearners.com

www.findaschool.org

www.geteducated.com/index.asp

www.program-online-degree.com

www.themoderndegree.com

www.worldwidelearn.com

There are many schools to choose from, and various programs will offer different credits for previously taken courses and/or work experience. Each school has its pros and cons, such as residency requirements, length of semesters, availability of classes, requirements for entrance exams, tuition, and overall reputation. We highly recommend you pursue a traditional university that offers online courses for your master's degree, if at all possible. It needn't be a well-known state university; it could be a small, private university, or even a faith-based one. This is not because we think less of the other nontraditional programs, but a master's from a traditional school will give you an edge as you begin your career teaching online. There are pros and cons whichever method you choose.

If you choose the traditional route for your master's, you will have a degree from a school that is easily recognized by those in the academic world as well as the corporate world, and it is more likely to be valued in the corporate world. Saying that you went to Pennsylvania State University will earn you a lot of respect, even if you took your courses online in a hybrid format or even totally online. Many business leaders are familiar with big-name schools that have strong sports programs but may be unfamiliar with one of the 100 percent online programs, such as Northcentral University, unless they knew someone who graduated from there. Your corporate resume will be easier to market when you don't have to explain that your school is real. This is, of course, assuming you want to stay in corporate America.

Second, you will stand out when applying to teach online. With the University of Phoenix producing more graduates than any other online university, you shouldn't be surprised to see that a significant number of applicants for teaching positions graduated from there. You will find yourself at a great advantage over the competition in part because you will be different. When schools recruit and hire online faculty, they aim for a diverse group from varied universities. A school's reputation will be lessened if it is known for essentially hiring its own graduates (inbreeding in academic circles is limited by accreditation bodies), and students will be more impressed to see some faculty from traditional universities. It gives the school and the teacher more credibility in students' eyes even though they are attending an online school. As a result, it will score you some bonus points in the application process.

Third, you can also choose to teach face-to-face courses. Traditional universities are hesitant to hire faculty with an online degree. Some don't respect the degree, others don't feel that you should deliver lectures when you weren't on the other end of them, and still others are just being difficult about wanting their faculty to come from schools just like theirs and be people who walked the same path. Earning a degree the traditional way, even including online courses, will give you easier entry into all realms of teaching. A purely online degree at the master's level will likely limit you to teaching only in online programs until you have proven yourself elsewhere. We're not saying it can't happen, only that having a master's from a traditional school, even if you took classes online, may look better for you; and in today's competitive world, any edge you can get is worth considering.

Wherever you earn your graduate degree, there are advantages to taking some or all of your courses online if you want to teach strictly online. If you're familiar with the difficulties online learners face, you will be more likely to understand your students. If you can articulate these clearly in a cover letter and resume, and note that your experience as a student has made you a better teacher, then this can be a strong plus in your corner. Since online schools know their own programs are credible, they won't hesitate to hire someone with a degree from an online institution. On-ground schools, however, will be less likely to hire you than if you had a degree from a traditional school.

If a traditional program is not an option for you, for whatever reason, then the next best recommendation is to pursue a nontraditional program that has a real campus, but one that also has an online component. For example, Webster University is an excellent option because of its shortened semesters, its 100+ campuses throughout the world, and its excellent online program. The school is traditional in St. Louis, where it has had its beautiful campus for over 80 years, but it is nontraditional everywhere else, so you get a lot of advantages. You might have difficulty landing a teaching job at a top-tier traditional university, but the rest are likely to welcome you.

If neither of these options works for you, then by all means get a master's somehow, but from a regionally accredited institution. Even if you go to a purely online school, just earn it. Focus on the time to completion, the reputation of the school, and the degree offerings. It wouldn't be worth your while to get a degree just to say you have one; a master of library science, while a real degree, will severely limit what you will be able to teach, while a master of information systems will enable you to teach any undergraduate computer science course anywhere. You should enjoy the subject you are studying, but you should also be sure that there are jobs for someone with that degree. If the degree you are pursuing is hard to find, then so will the openings for faculty in that area. Just remember that supply and demand go hand in hand. It's no wonder that business is the most commonly offered program and often has the best pay for full-time faculty.

Whatever method you decide to pursue, make sure it fits your lifestyle. This must be a priority if you want a real career teaching online and not just one or two courses on occasion.

With regard to our expert tips, what we've seen work, and what our colleagues say: We are proponents of schools with name recognition that also let you take courses online so you can explain that you understand the students' pain because you've been there. We also agree that if you intend to teach mostly on-ground or you want a high number of your courses to come from on-ground classes, you should opt for the more traditional route. This isn't based on statistics, but what we've seen work. Having experience with both on-ground and online courses will ultimately serve you best, as long as the school's degree is accredited and respected.

Enrollment

We discuss hunting for jobs extensively in Chapter 6, but here you can see which schools and programs have the highest enrollments. This will help you figure out which degree you may wish to pursue (you may want to go where the jobs are, or specialize) and may help you see where you want (or don't want) to attend. There are many lists available online, and the site you visit will largely dictate the answer you get with regard to which schools and programs have the highest enrollments. There are many ways to slice and dice the data, such as the number of students by parent company, United States alone, and so forth. Here are some you may want to consider, compiled from a variety of sources (this is not an endorsement of the schools, just an idea of who's out there):

- University of Phoenix—undisputedly the highest number of students; bachelor's degrees are available in business, management, information technology (IT), and health administration.
- American InterContinental University Online (AIU Online)—business, criminal justice, marketing, and visual communication.
- Kaplan University—criminal justice, IT, management, paralegal.
- DeVry University—business administration, IT, Computer Information Systems (CIS), technical management.
- Baker College—business administration, CIS, health services administration.
- Capella University—business, education, psychology, human services.
- Walden University—business, education, psychology, human services.
- Northcentral University—business, education, psychology.

You should also check out your local community college to see if it has online programs, as they are often a great entry into the world of online teaching because you get the benefit of local support when needed. You will undoubtedly find in your research that business is the most common program offered online. Those with a business degree have more opportunities for teaching than those with any other degree, based on enrollment and the availability of the major; however, you should note that they also have the greatest competition for those same teaching positions. The largest opportunities exist in the programs that are 100 percent online, but there are numerous schools that offer a choice of programs that may be good options for you to attend or teach at. Also, don't assume you are locked into teaching within your degree field. We both have degrees in business and yet have taught in schools of education.

Getting Your Doctoral Degree

Let's assume you either have your master's or are nearing completion of it and you have decided you want to pursue a doctorate. First, you should know that it's a long road that will be difficult, cumbersome, and full of trials; it will eat at your ego and sometimes even your self-esteem. It is a truly humbling process. Your education often seems to be at the mercy of others who are not nearly as invested in it as you are, and this can be troubling, anxiety-producing, and worrisome. There is good reason that only 50 percent of people who begin a doctorate ever obtain one (Coates, 2004). Your goal as a doctor is to help advance your discipline, to create social good, and to be a professional who is highly qualified in your field. If you were told that anything you'd pursue had a 50 percent rate of failure, you'd seriously reconsider doing it in the first place. Some consider it to be the fault of the educational system if students spend a great deal of money and effort only to have a 50 percent success rate. Remember, though, whether you reach your goal is entirely up to you, and also keep in mind that a doctorate qualifies you for jobs that no amount of experience or hiring quotas can.

Completion of Doctoral Programs

It's important to note that the number of Americans earning doctorates in the past five years has dropped more than 8 percent, yet again giving you an edge. (This is not true for foreign students, whose rate has risen by more than 5 percent in the same period of time—still a net loss result, making your degree more valuable.)

Here are some more interesting facts about doctorates: More than half who earn them do not stay in the teaching field. This clearly shows that they're universal in their demand, and that just because you earn a doctorate doesn't mean you can't go back to industry! As mentors, we realize that not everyone we mentor will go on to follow in our footsteps, leave their day jobs, and pursue academia along with some consulting. Many PhD programs are stepping up to the workplace challenge and are introducing programs that focus more on the practitioner than the school (called the practitioner-scholar approach as opposed to the scholar-practitioner approach). At the very least, in obtaining a doctorate you'll build an incredible network and understand research methodologies behind almost everything you see and do in modern life. How bad can it be? About 42,155 people found out in 2004 by earning their "terminal degree" (National Science Foundation, 2005). In 2003, 40,770 people earned the degree; 39,989 in 2002. More detailed statistics are available on the National Science Foundation's web site at www.nsf.gov. More than half of the doctorates were in science and engineering. The U.S. population as of March 2006 was 298,303,450, indicating that in 2004, roughly .014 percent of the population earned a doctorate (U.S. Census Bureau, 2006).

You can see now why a doctorate is in high demand at universities. If we look specifically at Americans who are at least 25 years of age (i.e., potential PhD candidates; there are very few exceptions who are eligible earlier), only 1.1 percent of these individuals have doctorates; 8.7 percent have a professional degree or a master's degree, and 17.2 percent of this population have a bachelor's degree. Only 3.1 percent of those with doctorates have an income at the poverty level (for various reasons, perhaps illness or choice), but this number is an astounding 10.6 percent for those who earned only a high school diploma (22.8 percent for those who didn't even complete high school). It's in your best interest to earn the highest degree you can, statistically speaking (U.S. Census Bureau, 2006). To work as an online teacher and make a lot of money, the best thing you can do is set yourself apart from your competition.

A doctorate will open up many worlds for you with regard to teaching opportunities. We prefer you go the online route for this degree; you can earn an accredited doctorate just as you would from an on-ground school. Traditional schools tend to have demands that are simply that, tradition, without regard for what actually makes sense and why it needs to be done. The point of a doctorate program is to know how to be a good researcher, understand the doctoral-level research methodology, have a thorough review of the literature in your field, and then be able to apply that to whatever you decide to do with hopes of making the world a better place, a more educated place to be. Any doctorate from an accredited school will give you an advantage here. The key is to decide if you want to earn a PhD, a DBA, an EdD, or some other doctorate and then to get it done. We'll review the most common doctorates in detail.

Doctor of Philosophy (PhD)

The doctorate of philosophy (PhD) can be in many subjects. The first formal PhD was instituted in 1893 in the field of education at Teachers College at Columbia University (Dill and Morrison, 1985). A PhD is a doctorate in philosophy in your area of specialization. PhD programs usually focus on preparing a candidate to perform specialized scholarly research. The emphasis here is on the development of new theory in various topics. Most PhD graduates work as university researchers and professors or as senior researchers in government agencies or businesses. The focus is often on being a scholar first and a practitioner second, although many programs today are emphasizing both to meet growing workplace demands.

Doctor of Business Administration (DBA)

The doctor of business administration (DBA) focuses on the application of theory rather than on the development of new theory. This in many ways exemplifies the practitioner-scholar model, while the PhD frequently exemplifies the scholar-practitioner model. By looking at it this way, you can clearly see the differences. A DBA often has more practical application for managerial settings than a PhD, but the two are very similar in other respects. They are considered academically equivalent and require difficult courses of study with a heavy research emphasis. Students must write and defend a doctoral dissertation in addition to passing comprehensive exams. Some schools now require any tenure-track faculty member to have a terminal degree (this is a doctorate) that's either a PhD or a DBA. Take heed that, while respected by the academic world, a DBA isn't quite as recognized by corporate America where it tends to be translated as database administrator. Also, a DBA is often a part-time commitment on the part of the learner (many DBA programs want you to remain employed full-time as they are professional-based).

Doctor of Education (EdD)

The first doctor of education (EdD) program came 27 years after the first PhD. The degree was established at Harvard University Graduate School of Education. The EdD prepares professional leaders to identify and solve complex problems. The emphasis in these programs is to develop reflective and competent practitioners who are thoughtful in nature. While the PhD focuses on research and producing new knowledge, the EdD focuses on career development and being the best professional possible. The EdD often pursues an administrative leadership role in educational institutions, whereas the PhD generally pursues scholarly practice, research, or teaching at the university level (New Mexico State University, 2005). If you want to be a credentialed psychologist, some insurance carriers won't qualify someone with an EdD but will qualify someone with a PhD or a doctorate of psychology (PsyD). This makes sense given the field; so ultimately, your end goal will determine which doctorate you should choose (and there are others; these are just the most common for online teachers).

Regardless of what you choose, accreditation matters. You need to pay particular attention to be sure your school is accredited and note the accrediting body. The doctoral degree, whichever types you pursue, is designed to be a rigorous and highly intellectual experience. You need to know what this feels like if you want to provide it to your own students. Most faculty members demand a lot from learners and you should be aware of this going in. Also, it's important to note here that once you make it to the dissertation phase, you're considered a doctoral candidate. At this point your unofficial status is referred to as "all but dissertation" (ABD). We hope you won't remain ABD for more than a year or two, but you can take advantage of this status when applying for teaching jobs. Many schools will see you as being almost a doctor, so they will often hire you as though you had your doctorate, but conditional on your actually finishing within a specified time. So it is important to mention your ABD status in your opening cover letter (discussed later in the book), as well as how far along in the process you are, because most likely the dissertation will be complete by the time you're hired.

In the next chapter, we talk about opportunities available to you regardless of the highest level of education you have reached.

4

Types of Online Teaching Jobs

There is an old saying that the course of civilization is a race be-tween catastrophe and education. In a democracy such as ours, we must make sure that education wins the race.

—John F. Kennedy

There are so many opportunities in the world of online teaching; this is truly an emerging field, growing rapidly and demanding quality individuals to teach at all university levels . In this chapter, we explore many of the opportunities and requirements of the online teaching world.

Experience—Needed or Not?

"No experience needed." How we long to see those words in a job advertisement when we are fresh out of school; but alas, you must have experience to get experience. It seems the only employers willing to hire you without experience are those with jobs that no one with a college degree would want anyway. We see that changing, and the world of online teaching is leading the way.

The world of online teaching is like uncharted territory. Although a few universities have been market leaders in distance education for a decade or so, most are just in the infancy stage. The demand for faculty to develop and teach their online courses far exceeds the supply, especially since most full-time professors have yet to teach online, and many don't want to. Keep in mind that traditional universities often expect research, grants, and such that require a doctorate. The same requirements are not evident in the online world. Adjuncts are needed more than ever before, and universities cannot afford the luxury of demanding experience since the supply of experienced online faculty cannot currently meet the demand. The ever-increasing cost of health care is also driving the need for adjuncts. As we discuss in the pros and cons section of the chapter, most if not all adjuncts do not receive benefits, which saves universities money.

What does this mean to you? It means that you can become an online professor without already being a professor. Experience will definitely help in getting hired where the competition is fierce, especially at the more prominent universities, but there are countless opportunities to get hired without experience and ultimately get the experience needed to move up the ladder to higher-paying and more prestigious positions. The best part is that it won't take years to pay your dues; within one year you can have enough experience to compete with anyone, provided you have the necessary academic credentials for that position.

However, just because you don't need teaching experience doesn't mean the borders are not guarded. One of the largest employers of online adjuncts is the University of Phoenix. This is an excerpt from its web site (www.phoenix.edu) on "Becoming a Faculty Member":

If you are a working professional with a graduate degree, in-depth knowledge of your field, strong communication skills, computer proficiency, and a desire to help others succeed, you may have what it takes to be a University of Phoenix Online instructor.

Here you see no mention whatsoever of teaching experience. American InterContinental University Online, another major employer of online faculty, shows the following on its web site (www.aiuonline.edu) with regard to "How to Apply for a Faculty Position":

> Prospective faculty members must meet the following criteria to be considered:
>
> Documented expertise in the academic subject area as well as interpersonal, oral presentation, and written communication skills.
>
> Minimum of two years of industry experience with prior postsecondary teaching experience preferred.

Here teaching experience is mentioned, but not as a requirement. This is typical. "Experience required" is now "Experience preferred, but must have graduate degree." Also note that industry experience is often seen instead of teaching experience. Chances are if you want to teach a subject, you are proficient in that subject due to either your academic qualifications or your professional experience, or both.

Why Do Schools Want Adjuncts?

Adjuncts have long been treated as road scholars by full-time faculty in traditional universities, often getting little or no respect. Their names are not included in most college catalogs, they don't have offices, they don't get invited to faculty functions, and they don't sit on stage during most graduations. While full-time faculty are a small but consistent cadre of professionals who account for a large percentage of the courses taught at these traditional universities, there is usually a large group of diverse adjuncts who account for the rest. Note that none of this is true for a fully online college like Walden University or Capella University, where there are far more adjuncts than full-time faculty and they are treated with equal respect and dignity, and adjuncts are usually invited to residencies, meetings, and faculty functions; in these nontraditional universities, most of the full-time faculty began as adjuncts there and it becomes difficult for students to distinguish between adjuncts and full-time faculty.

In any business, human resources are the biggest expense and often the most trying challenge to manage, so why not just hire a few more full-time instructors and eliminate the need for adjuncts?

The answers are plentiful, but the most obvious is simple economics. Adjuncts are a bargain, plain and simple. While a full-time faculty member can teach a full class and barely show a profit for the university, an adjunct can teach a small class and show a large profit. At one community college, the average full-time faculty salary is about $40,000 plus benefits per year, with a commitment to teach 10 courses. If benefits are estimated to be worth about $10,000 per year, then the salary package costs $50,000, so each course taught by a full-time professor costs the college $5,000. The tuition is $190 per yearlong course for state residents, so it takes 27 students in the class just to pay the professor's salary (and this doesn't include the building expenses or other administrative salaries).

An adjunct there earns $1,650 per course without benefits, so after nine students, the college has paid the adjunct's salary. With an average class size in the low to mid 20s, the college loses money with the full-time faculty and makes a significant profit with adjuncts, so the adjuncts make it possible to afford to keep full-time faculty.

Even in a nontraditional online university, such as Capella University, adjuncts are paid a set amount per student, so the university is guaranteed to show a profit regardless of the class size, while full-timers earn an annual salary and need to teach full classes to help the bottom line financially. Adjuncts are contractors, so they aren't paid benefits, sick time, vacation time, and the like.

Besides the monetary reasons, there are logistical reasons for wanting adjuncts. With rare exceptions, traditional universities have found it necessary to expand their market to include night and weekend students as well as online students. These are not popular options for most full-time professors, who don't want to work nights and weekends and may not even want to leave the comfort of their classrooms. Since adjuncts may have full-time jobs, making it difficult for them to teach during the weekdays, they are usually open to weekends and evenings. Full-time adjuncts work during the day like normal people, but are responsible for their own hours and maintaining their own schedules. Full-timers are left to handle daytime duties and other adjuncts are tapped for the rest. An added bonus to schools about using adjuncts for their online courses is the option to hire outside of the local community; there is no geographical restriction with regard to where an adjunct lives when teaching online, so the university can hire from anywhere in the world. From your standpoint as an adjunct, you can live in California or Florida and teach anywhere in the United States or even for international colleges.

Another factor to consider is that even the best of faculty have limited strengths. No one can teach everything, so universities are often left having to fill a few odd courses. If the unfilled courses on a schedule included one physics class, two psychology classes, and one Japanese class, it would be easier to hire three or four adjuncts to cover these than to find one person with the credentials for all of these.

Administratively, an adjunct is also a dean's dream. Adjuncts are easy to hire, easy to fire, and easy to reassign. Since adjuncts are contractors who essentially work for themselves, they are more willing to do whatever is asked of them since they are paid for what they do, and they want to stay on good terms to get more future assignments.

The more enlightened university leaders in the online world have come to look at adjuncts beyond the cost savings and course scheduling advantages. Schools like Capella University (www.capella.edu) and Walden University (www.walden.edu) proudly display the names of their entire faculty on their web sites, including adjuncts, who make up a majority at those schools. Adjuncts, with academic credentials equal to those of full-time traditional faculty, provide.pockets of expertise and add validity to the degree because of the well-roundedness of the diverse faculty.

What Types of Positions Are Available Online?

The first position available online, as has been mentioned earlier, is that of the adjunct faculty member. Adjunct faculty members teach classes on contract and are usually not employees. They are free to set their own schedules within the guidelines of the university they work for; they are contractors. As such, they manage their time but in return they do not have the job security that the full-timers have. They cannot be on a tenure track like full-time core faculty. They also do not receive benefits, but they do have flexible schedules and can make a lot of money working from home or while on any trips they choose to take.

Another opportunity is as a course developer. Every university has two things that need to be done routinely—course development and course revision. Course development involves creating a brand-new course, usually with a template and a textbook. It can pay anywhere from $1,000 to $5,000, depending on the university and the level of work required. Course revisions are minor or major updates to existing courses, and can pay anywhere from a few hundred to a couple of thousand dollars. This is usually an additional option adjunct faculty have; however, some universities will hire individuals who are experts in that area just to revise courses.

Another opportunity is that of lead faculty. Surprisingly, an adjunct/contractor can in fact become a lead faculty; this means you're responsible for updating the course regularly, and sometimes for assigning who will teach a course—so you get right of first refusal on the course, which means that you are asked to teach it before anyone else. This is a guarantee and will help you increase your income substantially, not to mention that it provides some level of job security.

There are even adjunct faculty members who hold paid positions in the hierarchy of a department. At Northcentral University (www.ncu.edu), adjuncts oversee the different majors in the School of Education. The responsibilities include overseeing all of the courses in the department and the faculty assigned to those courses; also, department chairs play a major role for students majoring in their subject area, as they may review some dissertations, too. The best benefit, though, is the ability to decide for yourself what your teaching schedule will be.

Requirements of Various Programs

While each university has its own specific rules and requirements, there are some core requirements common to almost all of them. If you are applying to teach at a regionally accredited institution, then it will likely insist that you have your graduate degree from a regionally accredited institution. The standards are somewhat more lax at nonaccredited institutions, so if your degree isn't from an accredited college, you should look for these online using searches.

The degree is just the beginning, though. You must have a graduate degree with at least 18 graduate semester hours in the subject area you plan to teach. For example, to teach finance, you wouldn't qualify with just an MBA that has one or two finance courses, but the MBA would certainly qualify you to teach general business or management. By taking all of your elective courses in a single subject area, you better prepare yourself to teach in that subject area. It is not uncommon for graduates to go back and take a few extra courses in order to meet minimum qualifications for teaching a favorite subject. If you get a second degree, whether it is another master's or a doctorate, it is the combined graduate courses that count, so you don't have to get all of your credits from a single institution—just be sure they are both accredited. Even those of you with a bachelor's degree can teach online at high schools as well as some universities, albeit mostly college preparatory courses or noncredit courses, due to strict accreditation guidelines; you'll want to review the requirements at several schools to find out which ones would allow you to teach with a bachelor's degree. Many will take a bachelor's degree with exceptional work experience for weeknight on-ground courses or an online course here or there while you're working on your master's.

Types of Online Teaching Jobs

The traditional university setting of teaching live classes in lecture halls is often known for the "publish or perish" mentality. Faculty members are required to get published in major academic journals annually or risk losing their jobs. Having a reputation as well-published carries more weight than being the best instructor, since it is through publishing that these universities gain status. The nontraditional university settings are quite different. Publishing is not a requirement, although it is very welcome and highly regarded. Online teaching is mostly populated by adjuncts, and adjuncts are contracted to teach classes almost exclusively. Thus, your history of getting published may help you get hired, but it is certainly not expected or required. You won't even be paid more for doing so.

With the adult learner environment prevalent in online education, more and more universities are requesting practical experience in the field of study being taught. The new model for teaching is that the instructor should be able to help students see real-world applicability, and this requires knowledge beyond the books. Additionally, it gives a different form of credibility to the university and the instructor when the students can read an instructor bio filled with real-world accomplishments.

For a prospective teacher, probably the most critical requirement of any online educational program, whether stated or not, is the ability to communicate. In a lecture hall, a professor must be able to communicate orally to be effective, but online education requires that a professor be able to communicate in written form as well. While this seems less challenging at first glance, it is quite the opposite. You will take courses on how to use proper tone, how to effect change, how to articulate well, and many other topics—all challenges for anyone who teaches online. Can you recall the last time someone took your e-mail wrong? In the online world there are no nonverbal clues other than perhaps emoticons to tell expression. This is an art form that you will become great at.

There are differences in how one should communicate in replying to an e-mail, in giving directions for online assignments, in grading papers submitted electronically, and in moderating a discussion forum. While there is no official certification for how one can communicate effectively, the process of applying to teach online is an opportunity for the university administration to assess some of your skills. Unlike a face-to-face or phone interview, your written word is permanent and can be read again and again, so check your resume, cover letter, and e-mail for typos, writing errors, and overall tone. Be sure your writing communicates what you want to communicate. We have provided some samples in Chapter 6.

Online High Schools

For those without master's or doctoral degrees, one road worth exploring is teaching online high school. You may not have heard of such a thing, but we can assure you that they are out there.

A high school diploma is a necessary step toward achieving success. The U.S. Department of Labor's Bureau of Labor Statistics indicates that the average high school graduate in 2002 earned about $717 per month more than the average person who had not completed high school. The gap is widening year after year. High school graduates are 70 percent more likely to be employed than those without a diploma.

In the past, a general equivalency diploma (GED) was the primary alternative to finishing high school. The GED is an exam comprised of five areas: writing skills, social studies, interpreting literature, science, and math. Completion does not give the student a high school diploma; they are a "GED holder." A high school graduate is of greater significance in our society than a GED holder. As a result, online schools quickly wised up and created online high schools, accredited institutions offering diplomas online.

You probably want some names—examples of online high schools. Here is a list in random order (and you will see that even the oldest of schools is embracing the idea): Penn Foster High School (established in 1890); James Madison High School; Keystone National High School (established in 1974); Orange Lutheran High School, Advanced Academics (middle school, too!); Apex Learning; Florida Virtual High School;

Brenton Academy; Brigham Young University; Christa McAuliffe Academy (regionally and nationally accredited!); Home Study International; Kentucky Virtual High School; University of Nevada Reno Independent Study; University of Texas at Austin; University of Oklahoma Independent Learning High School. You name your criteria; they are probably out there.

Throughout the book we mention several great web sites that will help you find online teaching jobs and available positions. Keep in mind that just because a school isn't advertising its need for faculty doesn't mean it doesn't have such a need! Follow the same steps we offer for beginning a career in online education, but adapt your resume to the high school level. The possibilities are endless and growing rapidly.

What Do You Need to Begin?

First, you need a desire to teach others. You need to want to share your experiences with others. Remember, online teachers are often referred to as facilitators—and that is what you do as an online teacher. Your students often have as much or more experience than you have, and they want respect and credit for that experience, not to be treated like typical college students who probably don't have responsibilities outside of schoolwork and play. It's essential for an online teacher to adopt the mind-set of facilitator/mentor rather than lecturer/teacher. Once you have that down and realize the differences, you can begin looking for online jobs.

Next, you need a degree in something from an accredited institution. If you're lucky, your degree is also in your chosen work field; if it is, matching yourself to courses and qualifying to teach will be much simpler. However, most of us are the result of several changed majors and perhaps even a career change or two. Begin to document what you want to teach in general (management, finance, economics, statistics, IT, etc.) and why you are qualified to teach it. These details need to be captured when you regularly update your resume as well as the cover letter you use to apply for teaching positions.

You need to have the necessary technology, as is discussed in Chapter 10. Don't just have the right equipment; also make sure you have Internet access readily available, even if it means walking to a local coffee shop if you lose service at home.

Finally, you must have good intentions. We can't emphasize enough that teaching online or on-ground is a tremendous responsibility, both to your colleagues and to your students. If your goal is to get rich quick and put in little effort, you are in the wrong field. This is hard work, but it's rewarding and you can make a lot of money with tremendous flexibility. However, your good intentions are vital to your success and your presentation style. As dedicated professors, we tend to police ourselves, and those who don't have the right attitude about teaching will find that their colleagues won't network with them. We have successfully helped dozens of friends and former students get jobs as online professors, but our reputations are on the line when they don't perform, so we will recommend only those who would do us proud. Likewise, we have received job opportunities because of others who have liked our work, often without our having to ask. Once this noble profession is overrun by entrepreneurs who don't care about students but only about fast money, the quality will drop and so will enrollment, and ultimately teaching opportunities will diminish. So remember that, while the money is good, the work is real and demanding of your time.

Upsides and Downsides to Adjunct Life

Adjunct life has its upsides and its downsides, as all jobs do. Many adjuncts aspire to become full-time professors, while others are content to remain adjuncts. Some work full-time in their profession and use adjunct work as a supplement to their income, whereas others choose to do it full-time.

You may also choose one path and then change mid-course. You may decide you like teaching online, or you may not.

Compensation is definitely a key issue. A full-time professor can expect to make at least $40,000 plus benefits annually to teach 5 to 10 courses per year, whereas an adjunct might earn only $2,000 to $3,000 without benefits for a single course. Mathematically, you would need to teach more than twice what a full-timer teaches to earn the same amount. This may be true on the surface, but there are hidden truths, too. Full-time faculty must often serve on committees, attend meetings, teach courses they don't want to teach on a schedule they may not like, and often publish in journals, while adjuncts just teach (possibly attending a rare conference call). Adjuncts are afforded more time to teach more classes. Additionally, adjuncts get paid only for what they do, and can take a term off or lighten their load for a vacation. They get paid for everything they attend that is student related, and almost no meeting is mandatory. There is no limit to how much adjuncts can earn since they are contracted employees who get paid for what they do, and an efficient adjunct professor who can stay organized can handle many classes simultaneously at multiple universities. Now with the all-too-common shortened semesters in adult learning environments, it is not surprising to find adjuncts teaching more than 50 classes per year without restrictions, thus putting earnings potential at well over $100,000 per year working few hours or over $200,000 per year choosing to work full-time and serve on paid dissertation and comprehensive exam committees and attend paid academic residencies that learners are often required to attend.

Benefits are a major concern these days, and many professionals are afraid to leave their employers because of losing benefits.

There are two key benefits to employees that drive their job decisions above all else—vacation days and medical insurance. As an adjunct professor, your vacations are officially unpaid, but they are under your control. It is possible to take vacations while teaching, reducing workload systematically those days but still logging in, and catching up when returning. You are essentially taking vacations while earning pay. Adjuncts are automatically on unpaid vacation when classes are not in session, and they can choose not to teach for a semester (without pay), or, if permitted, they can have a colleague log in for them for a few days and handle their online courses (provided they are teaching at the same university with relevant knowledge of the material). Note: We are not advocating this, though it's frequently done when the adjunct teaches at the same school or university and has the same qualifications. Check with your own online colleges to find out the rules first! They will often work with you if you are up-front with your issues; they often ask adjuncts to cover for a full-timer for a week while that person is on a cruise or giving birth or attending a funeral.

As for health insurance, undoubtedly the most expensive benefit to lose, there are many reasonably priced plans available to self-employed individuals. When one of these plans is coupled with the Health Savings Account, adjunct professors can feel secure that they are covered sufficiently and there is no need to ever feel dependent on an employer to provide group health insurance. Taking on perhaps one or two additional classes per year can pay for an entire year of health care premiums.

Job security has also been a subject of concern for the past couple of decades. In the days of the nuclear family, a person could expect to stay with one company until retirement. Now, retirement is almost a fantasy, as most employer-funded plans are being eliminated and employees are left to maintain their own retirement plans. Universities are one of the rare places in which retirement plans are still strong, and tenured faculty are probably the only employees in the country who can feel comfortable knowing that they cannot easily be fired. Adjuncts are at the opposite end of the spectrum in that there is no true job security, there are no retirement packages, and it is easy to get fired (technically you don't get fired; you just don't get rehired).

So why be an adjunct? In reality, there is an innate sense of job security that is unsurpassed. Universities need adjuncts, and good ones are a valued commodity, often treated better than full-timers by the deans because we can easily leave, and they don't want us to. We can still supplement our income while consulting, and if we aren't rehired by one university, chances are we can relatively quickly be hired by another to make up the lost income.

Unlike many positions, if you do your job well you can feel secure that you will get hired again. You probably won't be outsourced, and you can go elsewhere at any time. You can add to your workload, and the universities can't ask you not to. In fact, you can teach at multiple universities at one time, thus creating a situation in which no one employer controls more than a limited percentage of your income. Try that in a full-time job! This is job security in the truest sense; it is based on your own work ethic and principles. How hard you work dictates how well you will be rewarded, and it is not at the whim of someone with less talent or education than you have. It is this principle that is the cornerstone of our plan in this book.

When you are teaching online, course setups are locked. Once you design a course as you wish, you can keep it that way forever (or until the textbook changes or, in the case of some types of IT courses, the technology changes). Typically, you can expect to invest significant time during your first run of a course, but the time drops dramatically the second time, and levels out on the third time. If you set up your courses right, you'll even have folders of data to post with it organized by the week you should post it. Experienced professors learn to improve their courses each time after noting confusing exam questions, poor discussion questions, and repeated e-mails on the same topic. It doesn't take long before the course is set to your satisfaction and the earnings feel almost effortless. Telling your department chairperson about the changes that need to be made in a course to help not only the students, but you, too, shows that you care about quality education. It's a win-win.

Now, here is a downside you must be aware of. Good luck ever having a real worry-free, nonworking vacation. Also, if you turn down a contract, then two things happen: (1) you don't get paid; (2) the school finds someone else to fill your shoes that term, and that person may end up filling them permanently. Turning down a contract is risky. One solution is to never turn one down, but that means true vacations will be rare. Unfortunately some universities are year-round with no breaks even for major holidays, so you truly don't get a day off. Significant others will need to be aware of this time commitment. Yes, you can work from anywhere, but you will have to work at least a few hours each day. Another solution is to make some minor schedule adjustments in a course to allow yourself a lighter week than normal, but the work is not completely gone and you must still reply to e-mails quickly. If you get burned out easily, this job is not for you.

What Is Required of Adjuncts at Most Schools?

There is no true standard on job requirements for an online adjunct faculty; however, there are certain requirements that are very common. What you would have to do depends on the online platform used, the university culture, the level of the course, the type of assignments in the course, the length of the course, the size of the class, whether the course is asynchronous, and whether you teach from a master template or get to design your own course. The combination of requirements for a university's online program weighs heavily into whether the pay is truly fair.

First and foremost, you can expect to go through an orientation and online training wherever you teach. These usually take a lot of time and are designed to indoctrinate you into the school culture while teaching you the online platform. They are usually not paid, so be prepared to invest time in your future. It is also an opportunity for the school to evaluate you before handing you a class of your own. You can expect the training to take as long as a standard course, so plan on a couple of months of training. Some schools, like Baker College (www.baker.edu), go the extra mile and have you spend a full term shadowing another instructor, too, so it takes two full terms before you can begin to earn money. Don't take these training courses lightly. You will be evaluated and judged based on your performance. A training course is not a guarantee of a contract position.

Online courses can be classified as synchronous or asynchronous. Synchronous courses require that the professor be online at the same time as the students, and chat rooms are heavily utilized; this means that during selected hours, the professor must log in and moderate a discussion actively. It is not uncommon for a school to ask the professor to schedule additional chats at different hours of the day to accommodate students in different time zones. One chat a week is often helpful if designed to answer everyone's questions at once, as it saves a lot of time in responding to multiple e-mails, but when it is just another graded discussion on top of all of the graded written discussions, it can begin to challenge your time management abilities and can quickly lessen the value of the salary earned at that school. Asynchronous courses are far more common, especially at the graduate level, as there are no chats and so each person can log in at any time, post a question or reply to a question, and wait a day for a response. Asynchronous classes offer far more flexibility for the learner and the adjunct.

Faculty meetings are not uncommon for online universities. Some will host one or two mandatory conference calls per quarter, some will host one or two per year, some will host them only when some major event occurs, and some never have such calls. Faculty meetings can be valuable since they keep you in touch with the school and the communication is much stronger, but excessive meetings can cut into your schedule, especially since the meeting times are not flexible. As with course chats, these hours must be factored into your decisions to work for a university, for no matter how efficient you are at grading assignments, these telephone hours cannot be shortened. In the beginning, don't ask and don't worry—just get the experience. Later, when you decide which universities you want to keep and which ones you don't, you can be selective based on these types of criteria. For now, just go with it.

While not common, don't be surprised if you are asked to have office hours. These are hours in which you must be reachable by phone and ready to reply to a student who calls. If you don't get many calls, you can get your work done, but you are still committed to being at the phone.

Some say "reachable," like Axia College, which means by e-mail, instant messaging, or phone.

Assignments vary dramatically by course. Often a quantitative course will have many small assignments that need quick feedback, while other courses may have only a few major assignments. Grading quantitative problems is more objective and often quicker to accomplish than grading research papers, which require editing, critical evaluation, and written feedback. With quantitative problems, a solutions file can be provided so students can check their work in light of your comments, whereas with research papers your comments stand alone and must justify any grade less than an A. Sometimes it is up to the instructor to set up assignments and other times the assignments are hard-coded into the course. Requirements on grading vary by school, but you can expect to have about three to five days to grade assignments after they are submitted. In budgeting your time, you should consider that the vast majority of students submit their assignments on the day they are due, so you will find yourself grading a lot at once if you are not careful. By adjusting the deadlines in different courses or giving incentives for early submission, you can manage your time better and be more responsive in grading so as to meet the school's time lines. If you do things right, you can even schedule one day off per week for yourself.

Discussion forums can be the easiest or the hardest part of the job. In some courses, the students get so involved in the weekly discussions that you as a moderator need only read them and add your two cents' worth as appropriate. You want to add something each day to show you are alive and actually reading their postings, and many universities will log in to make sure you're posting substantive posts based on their time frames. Axia College is notorious for this in the adjunct world, as is the rest of the University of Phoenix system. Others will let you do your job and base evaluations on your performance. When universities just want you to moderate the forums, the only challenges are picking good questions that will get the maximum participation and knowing how to get students to reply when they are not active.

At the opposite extreme, there are those universities that require you to comment to everyone; this means for every posting by a student, several other students must comment to that student, and you must comment to the original posting as well as the replies to that posting. Should any of them reply to you, you must reply again regardless of the status of the thread. The discussion thread grows exponentially as the class gets larger, and you are often scored by the school based on your quantity of postings. This can be a drain on your time if not kept in check, and yet it is often the basis on which the student defines whether a course is a good one or a bad one. This is one reason to start ranking your colleges by workload and pay as you acquire relationships with more of them.

E-mails for online courses should ideally be kept in the course room and not in your private e-mails. Regardless of how it is done, students expect quick responses and you are obligated to give them. You really need constant access to your e-mail; a personal digital assistant (PDA) with e-mail accessibility can make you available during office hours even if you're doing crunches at the gym. Often the university will mandate that you reply to student e-mails within 24 hours. In more difficult courses, you can expect more e-mails from students crying out for help, and that takes up immeasurable time. As you go through a course, you'll learn what questions are asked and may find creative solutions, like a frequently asked questions (FAQ) document that helps learners be self-directed. Often you will see the same questions from several students, and if you reply to everyone at once in the main discussion forums you can eliminate many repeated questions. The key here is to minimize the need for students to send e-mails since they are unplanned and urgent by definition.

In a nutshell, a university will place requirements on you in terms of responsiveness, specific hours to be available, and visible proof of your work posted in the course rooms. These vary from school to school, and often you won't get the full picture until you actually teach for the school, so be open to anything.

Time Is Money: Balancing the Load and Evaluating Your Real Rate of Return

So you have decided to teach online, and you are just applying everywhere. You receive an offer and the pay sounds great, but is it? Time is money, and you must consider that fact above all else. You will often find schools paying a little more than industry average but demanding a lot more than average in terms of work, making it worth less than you might think. Sometimes you will take less pay because you need the experience, there are some nice perks, or they treat you well or let you teach something you enjoy a lot; but you must weigh everything—above all, your time. Since the only other measurable factor in the decision making process besides pay is one's time, let us treat that as the primary factor for our purposes.

When you get into a routine, you could potentially be in the discussion forum less than 15 minutes per day, depending on the number of discussion questions, the size of the class, and the commenting requirements. In schools where the requirements are stringent, you might find yourself in the discussion forum for closer to an hour per day, possibly more. Thus you might be committing to two to seven hours per week. Some online schools actually require the professors to grade the discussions each week, and that adds more time to your weekly commitment.

Grading assignments can take a serious chunk of time, too. One popular online school will typically give you classes of 35 students with three assignments per week, so you would be grading 105 papers per week, each requiring detailed comments. You might find yourself spending at least 20 hours per week reading these papers. The same popular online school mandates three hours of chats per week and holds biweekly conference calls. Combined with the hours spent on discussions and assignments, a professor can expect to spend 30 hours per week on a single class. So a salary of $2,000 per five-week course really amounts to only $13 per hour—not worth it to most of us.

A lesser-known community college that pays $1,600 for eight weeks' work is actually a better deal. A general business course there has weekly objective exams that are automatically graded, so the professor invests zero minutes per week (unless glitches occur). Discussions do not require rigorous commenting, so only about two hours per week are needed there. Learners are expected to be self-directed. The courses are asynchronous, so chats are nonexistent. Other than unplanned e-mails, a professor can expect to spend about three or four hours per week on the course, thus earning about $60 per hour. This is quite different from a course that appears to pay more money for a shorter semester. What's important is that you figure out what is worth your time and budget accordingly.

How Many Schools Should You Work For?

There is no limit to how many schools you can work for. One of the benefits of being a contractor is that you are not restricted from working anywhere. If you're good, you may at some point be offered a core faculty position. While this is an honor and a reflection of your hard work and dedication, you usually can't work for the competition; this means you may take a great pay cut.

Often a school may give you a lot of work, and you may feel that it is enough work to satisfy you, but then you are in a precarious position. A full-time faculty member has some degree of job security; by contrast, an adjunct can be released easily without notice. A talented and experienced adjunct should have no trouble finding another position, but it takes time to get processed, trained, and scheduled. By having at least three active schools, you will never feel pressured to do what you don't wish to do for fear of being unemployed. Knowing that you always have some form of income puts you in control. The more schools you are employed with, the more easily you can choose to quit some less profitable ones (or those you just don't like) and trade up in an effort to maximize your income for your invested time. Just don't do more than you can handle, for you wouldn't want a reputation for doing substandard work—that is a death sentence in adjunct life.

Personality, Strengths, and Marketing Yourself

It's important that the job you are doing matches your personality. If you are wanting to quit your day job because you don't like having to be there by 9 A.M. when you suffer night after night from insomnia, you won't like a synchronous class that makes you log in at a certain time. If you want more set office hours and want to feel as though your job isn't just dangling in the wind requiring time throughout all hours of the night, then you will like a synchronous format more. If you like sitting in front of your computer and prefer e-mails to phone calls, then choose universities that don't require conference calls and that let you respond primarily, if not entirely, by e-mail.

Determine what traits you like in a job and which ones you dislike. Make sure the online colleges you eventually work for, once your teaching resume is built, reflect your personality. If you don't, say hello to burnout and a simultaneous hello to job change.

You will also need to determine what your strengths are to market yourself. While an entire section in the book is devoted to this, briefly: This means figuring out your best qualities and selling them to universities. Are you a fast responder? If yes, then talk about your responsiveness and demonstrate your responsiveness by replying to letters of inquiry within a couple of hours and completing and faxing back paperwork the same day it's sent to you. If you prefer phone communications, you may ask for a voice interview to help your strengths shine through. If you are a writing expert, be sure your e-mails show this. If you are passionate about a topic, be sure that comes across. Understanding yourself and your personality is key to being happy in adjunct life and to being hired by new schools.

5

How Much Can
I Earn?

You can pay people to teach, but you can't pay them to care.
—Marva Collins

When we talk with individuals in groups, no one wants to ask this question, nor answer it. But when we talk one-on-one with people who want to earn a living teaching online, the question almost certainly comes out in the open: "So, how much can I make teaching online?" You can earn anywhere from a few hundred extra dollars monthly to a six-figure salary, depending on how much work you want to do and if you want this to be your full-time career or just extra income.

Several factors influence what you are paid to teach an online course. Remember that teaching is only one of several ways to make money working for an online school. In this chapter we talk about factors influencing your pay, what kind of paycheck to expect for an online course, and then additional ways to make money.

What Influences Your Pay?

This list is not all-inclusive, but reflects what our experiences have been regarding pay. It's important to note that usually the pay is not negotiable. This means that you're made an offer; if the school really wants you, it may budget a few extra dollars, but the pay basically is what it is. Many schools are for-profit and some are even public entities. They must adhere to budgets and profit and loss (P&L) projections just like the rest of corporate America. We've found less negotiating room for online courses than in our day jobs! If you are unhappy with the pay offered, you may suggest that with your qualifications you expected a little more, but be forewarned—this is not looked upon very highly. Usually if you don't like the pay, just don't take the job. We recognize that sometimes, especially in the beginning, you may have to take what you can get. Try to keep in mind that this is only until you build up your reputation.

- *The school you teach for.* Each and every school, and sometimes each and every program within a school, offers a different pay rate. Just like in traditional models, some schools are known for attracting top talent by paying top dollar. Others set a wide net and hope they catch some excellent teachers for smaller numbers. When looking for courses to teach online, don't hesitate to ask about money once mutual interest is shown. (Don't do this, of course, within the first few correspondences.) Since pay rates change constantly and out of respect for the universities we are affiliated with, we won't talk specifically about which schools pay us the most, but you will soon find out. Think prestigious = larger paycheck; less prestigious = smaller paycheck.
- *The level of the degree program.* Generally, you are paid in order of degree hierarchy; doctoral degree programs pay the most, then master's, then bachelor's, then associate. This is not a hard-and-fast rule, but it is the typical scenario.

- *Your credentials.* You don't have much negotiating room, but the initial offer may vary depending upon your own credentials. You will earn more for a more advanced degree, as we said, or for more teaching experience. If the school is recruiting you away from another university, this is even better.
- *Your role.* If you are a course lead, expect to be paid better. If you are a subject matter expert (SME), expect slightly higher pay.
- *The number of students in your course.* Some schools pay per student. In fact, some are even "check in, check out" systems where there is no real discussion thread, only assignments you must log in, check out, and grade. These institutions usually pay per student. If you have an oversized class, expect an "over limit" fee. This also varies by university.
- *The course you are willing to teach.* This isn't usually advertised, but at some schools the courses that are hard to recruit for sometimes pay more. You have no way of knowing which ones these are, and it's awkward to ask; but this is something to keep in mind.
- *Length of the term.* The longer terms typically pay more; however, it's best to document how much time you spend for each class versus the pay and determine an hourly rate so you can make decisions later on regarding which ones to continue working for and which ones to end relationships with.
- *Faculty development.* Many schools have created courses to teach faculty subjects like how to write a syllabus, how to mentor, or how to use e-mail effectively. Some of these faculty development courses are mandatory to complete before you are assigned a course to teach, but often a school will have several optional courses and will pay you more money for having completed the series. The pay increase may be substantial or only nominal, but often there is a greater gain in that you are seen as a serious team member and may be given more opportunities to teach.

What Can I Expect to Make for My Work?

From our experience, pay for a six-week class can range from $1,000 to $3,000. How much time one course takes you to teach will depend on whether you've taught it before, your experience teaching online, and the particular demands of that university. You will want to document this as you begin working because eventually you may have to make decisions regarding which universities are worth your while, and which ones aren't.

Longer classes warrant additional pay; but keep in mind, as noted earlier, that the pay may not translate to a larger hourly wage. For 12-week courses, expect anywhere from $1,800 to $5,000, depending on your role (instructor, faculty lead, rank) and the university. You can easily see how multiple courses can begin adding up to a sizable income. Remember, though, most likely you will be a contract employee, a status that has even less stability than employment at will. Your contract is usually for one term (6 weeks, 12 weeks, etc.) at a time! The job stability can be high if you are good, but not so high if consistently get bad student reviews.

If you are being paid per student, expect anywhere from $125 to $300 per student per course. Sometimes, while the amounts seem small, being paid per student actually means you earn more money than you would in a typical online classroom setting, so don't discount these opportunities without researching them.

If you are developing a new course, you can expect to be paid $1,000 to $4,000. This is a one-time payment for the course; once you turn over the materials the school usually owns the copyright. While this doesn't mean you can't use some of your own material elsewhere, it does mean you cannot copy and paste the course for another school and get paid twice for the same work—this is not acceptable practice and can get you into a lot of trouble. Remember, one major advantage to developing a course is you can often ask for right of first refusal for teaching it.

If you are revising or updating a course, expect anywhere between $500 and $2,000. Usually this is less time intensive than developing a new course. It typically will not lead to a right of first refusal for teaching, although it does often reflect positively on your work if you turn your course in on time and work well with the course development team. Each university has a different process for this. Some let you "go develop" right into the system! Others require a long process, a course you must take, and lots of approvals. Obviously you will want to be paid more for the time-consuming ones, so you need to find out what is required before you accept an offer.

If you are a lead and are expected to make minor revisions, keep others apprised of your work efforts, and help recruit faculty, add anywhere from $2,000 to $10,000 per year per area you're responsible for. Usually if you are a lead for only one class you'll be on the low side of that number; if you're responsible for multiple courses within a program, then expect to be on the higher side.

How to Make Extra Money

There are lots of ways to make extra money teaching online. We have already mentioned several pay opportunities. Another way is to make yourself an invaluable resource for the university. Attend faculty events so that they know you are interested and invested; offer to take on free tasks now and again; and whatever you do, don't whine about your workload! It's acceptable to make comments about oversized classes if a situation is impacting the students' learning, but avoid making comments like "You aren't paying me enough"; it is a surefire way to get the boot next term. While these things won't directly improve your pay, they will keep you on the "top dog" list, which means that when pay raises come up, you're likely to be one of the people who get one.

If you've been working for a school for years and you haven't been given any raises, it's appropriate to ask your boss if pay raises are available and, if so, what one should do to be considered for one. Then explain what you've done to help the school and that you are invested in the future and in it for the long haul, and proceed to ask for a modest raise. Remember these schools operate on tight budgets, so what you perceive as a small gesture may in fact be a big deal. This is important to recognize because you don't want to get a reputation for being a complainer or ungrateful. Also, remember that if you live in California and the school is in Michigan, you may be paid Michigan wages despite your higher living costs. This means you may need to work more than your counterparts to pay your bills, but that is a decision you have to make regarding your own lifestyle.

Another way for you to make additional money is to let your chairperson or deans know that you're willing to take on last minute classes. Sometimes, due to a family emergency, illness, crisis, or unreliability, schools have to reschedule courses or find a new instructor at the last minute. If you're willing and able to take on classes at the last minute, you may have an opportunity to make additional money. Once you begin teaching for a school, make it clear what other subjects you want to teach and are qualified to teach, and explain why, using criteria like credit hours in a subject or professional experience. Be sure to wait until you've built up a good reputation at a school before asking for more work. You want to prove yourself first.

Another option is to ask to teach faculty workshops, be a faculty trainer (be forewarned: this is a lot of work!), or be a quality auditor. Usually this requires that you spend some time going through courses and checklists to be sure faculty members are doing their jobs.

If you can write a book that would benefit the students, you might be able to sell your work through the school. Not only is there a large profit margin, but the author is seen as more of an expert by the school, and the school directly helps with the sales. Also, since you will be in the academic world, you should contact major textbook publishers and let them know that you are available to review textbooks. They will often pay $250 to $1,000 to review a textbook, depending on the work involved. Your credentials as a professor will carry weight in being selected for this privilege, so wait until you are actually teaching before seeking these opportunities.

6

The Hunt: Finding Your First Job

Anyone who stops learning is old, whether at twenty or eighty. Anyone who keeps learning stays young.

—Henry Ford

Finding jobs online is the key to successfully beginning your online teaching career or adding jobs to your existing career. Throughout this chapter, we explore several successful techniques that are new and creative but, more important, are proven strategies. First, though, you have to find the university and program you're both qualified for and interested in teaching in. There are many resources you can use to find online universities, and there are literally hundreds of them.

Locating Schools

Ask your colleagues, friends, teachers, or anyone you know who may teach online. Find online instructors, who often create links to their clients (the schools that they teach for). Remember the online teacher is an entrepreneur, running a small business with one or more clients, all of which are the universities and students that they serve. Create a top 10 list of colleges you'd like to work for and—contrary to logic—e-mail them *last*. You want to practice—see what works and what doesn't—and you don't want to do this on your top choices. You'll be amazed at how many modifications you make to your introductory message before you feel really good about it. Use the rejections and think through the introduction and resume several times before you send it to your top 10 school list. Still, don't wait *too* long; time is of the essence.

There are also lots of tools you can use online to find schools. Sites such as Adjunct Nation and even Monster.com show not only schools but also lots of open online teaching jobs. Both provide lists of opportunities, and you should apply through the mechanisms outlined in the job postings as well as the methods we describe in this chapter. Do not just follow the rules. The rules won't always get you visibility—you may be put into a database along with other people who never get looked at. After all, the responses to job postings are typically filed by human resources (HR) clerks and not by the well-educated deans, so you may be screened out because a clerk incorrectly judged you unqualified. Here is a list of places that list more schools than you can imagine:

info.theonlinedegree.com

www.adjunctnation.com

www.chronicle.com

www.degreeinfo.com

www.educationcenteronline.org

www.elearners.com

www.findaschool.org

www.geteducated.com

www.program-online-degree.com

www.themoderndegree.com

www.worldwidelearn.com

Finding Programs to Teach In

Go to the web sites of schools on your list and figure out which programs you are qualified to teach for and what looks interesting. You will need to list the courses you feel qualified for and interested in teaching in your introductory e-mail. This is usually the first thing the person receiving your e-mail asks; in addition, the fact that you are prepared and knowledgeable about the university's programs will come across in your e-mail message. This is important, because you don't want to appear as though you are just spamming universities to find jobs. Remember that you aren't spamming— you are offering important services to students and you are qualified to do so. The programs will offer their course lists and the descriptions; be prepared to answer follow-up e-mails about why you are qualified to teach in the programs you indicated in your message. Often a school has a need to fill a specific course, and if your letter mentions that course you will be more likely to stand out than someone whose resume must be read to determine if he/she is qualified to teach that course. And don't just use course names; use the school's own course numbering system. After all, wouldn't it be more impressive to state that you would like to teach STA1234—Business Statistics than to merely state that you teach statistics?

Hierarchy's Role in Finding Your Contact

Universities generally have several layers of bureaucracy, and online organizations, which are often public companies, may have even more than the norm. After you navigate to a prospective employing university's contact page, find the link for applying as an adjunct faculty member. If there isn't one, then find HR's e-mail address; it's usually on the contact page somewhere. Send your cover letter in the body of your e-mail and attach your resume or your curriculum vitae (CV) to the very first introductory e-mail. Later in this chapter we provide examples of what your introductory letter may look like, as well as sample academic resumes. Using the words "curriculum vitae" is just academia's way of asking for a resume that goes a bit beyond the standard information and is not limited to one page as a professional resume often is. It just means you can elaborate more with regard to the courses you have taught, the skills you have, the graduate credits you have earned, and the work you have published.

Human Resources

The obvious answer to finding jobs online is to contact the human resources department. However, just as direct contacts in the business world prove more effective in increasing your visibility than going through traditional methods, so is going directly to those hiring at online colleges. First, however, we'll discuss the human resources method. Some universities will require you to use this method regardless, so it's worth covering despite it being less effective for visibility within the right levels of the organization.

Even if you submit your resume directly to a contact, as we outline in the next section, you should submit it to HR; you may be asked to do this anyway, so it will save time. It also may lead to the department chairperson receiving your resume twice within a couple of days—not a bad reminder of your interest.

Keep the introductory letter to human resources generic, beginning with "Dear Human Resources:"; however, be certain it has the same data as the e-mail you send directly to contacts. You do not want to have any lack of clarity regarding your qualifications.

Direct Contacts

We firmly believe that finding direct contacts is the best way to get jobs in academia, particularly in online schools. As in business, introducing yourself directly to the hiring manager is a very effective way to be seen, as well as to show the dedication, perseverance, and self-direction it takes to directly contact hiring managers. Understanding the hierarchy at these institutions is critical. Unlike businesses, though, schools often put their faculty, department chair, and school dean e-mail addresses online. If they don't, it's relatively easy to find out what they are.

Usually, faculty members report either to a lead faculty for a specialization of study or directly to a department chair. This often depends on how big the institution is and whether it's serving a large student population, whether it's a public or private company, and the size of the school you want to work for. A university is comprised of numerous schools (areas of study like management, public health, or human services) and then areas of specialization within those schools, like information systems management, preventative care, or social work. Faculty chairs are often responsible for specializations, and deans are responsible for entire schools. A business school dean has several faculty chairs reporting to him or her, and the faculty report to the chair or a lead. A typical hierarchy is shown in Figure 6.1 (in some schools, there is a chief academic officer or provost between the president and the deans).

Using Direct Contacts

Looking at the diagram it's easy to see where you need to look and who you need to contact. If you're used to working in industry, you could replace the department chairpersons with managers or directors; however, you would rarely find their e-mail addresses published. Universities generously provide contact information—a huge benefit if you are looking for a job. After you have found a university you want to work for, follow

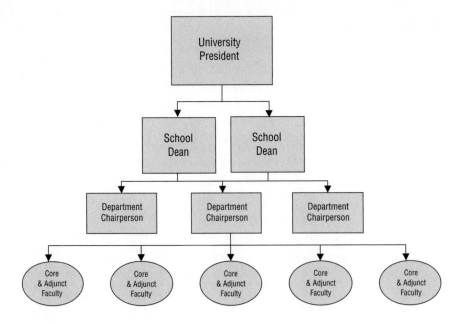

Figure 6.1 **Institutional Hierarchy**

these steps for locating and then introducing yourself to the appropriate individuals:

1. Look for the programs you are interested in working for (and qualified to teach in!).

2. Review the web sites and determine who the department chairpersons and/or the school deans are. Note their first and last names and their degrees, if posted. If degrees aren't posted, it's safest to assume that individuals have doctorates and address them formally as such. If you reach someone who doesn't have a doctorate, at worst you have called someone who isn't a doctor a doctor; this is not nearly as offensive as calling a doctor "Miss" or "Mister."

3. Compose an introductory message (see the "Sample Documents" section of this chapter) and address it to the individual you want to work for, starting off with "Dear Dr. Such and Such." Keep it a formal introductory opening, and then let your personality shine in the rest of your e-mail.

4. The subject line needs to make it clear you are job hunting. However, if you are a referral, that also needs to be clear. We recommend one of the following subjects:

   Adjunct Introduction: Online Teaching

   Referral—Adjunct Online Position

5. Blind carbon copy (BCC) yourself. This will help you keep track of everyone you have e-mailed and will make it easier to follow up. Since often it takes two to three months to even get a response, you will want to follow up and keep track of who suggested you write back at a later time. An Excel spreadsheet or an e-mail folder can easily accomplish the organization required to do this.

6. If you are sending the e-mail to a department chairperson, carbon copy (CC) the dean. If the chair has changed positions, CC-ing the dean saves time and reduces the potential for error, but also shows that you respect the hierarchy and know you'd be working for the chairperson.

What if the e-mail address of the person you need to contact isn't listed? It is rare but does happen that the university lists the contact name but not the e-mail address. You have a really good chance of still getting an e-mail through if you use the following technique.

Most companies use one of several naming formats, simply because it's easier for technical support people and creates logical name directories for internal employees. The most common naming conventions are:

FirstInitialLastName@universityname.edu (e.g., JTestUser@university name.edu)

FirstName.LastName@universityname.edu   (e.g.,   Joe.TestUser@ universityname.edu)

Lastname@universityname.edu (e.g., TestUser@universityname.edu)

If you don't know the individual's e-mail address, look at other e-mail addresses listed on the technical support page, the student recruitment page, or the HR page to ascertain the domain name. If it says @university name.edu for these departments, chances are the same domain name is used for all individuals who work for the university. You can deduce the first part of the e-mail address in the same way. For instance, if the employment department has an e-mail address of Jan.TestUser@university name.edu, then you can be quite certain the school uses the FirstName .LastName@universityname.edu format.

Now here is the key: You do not want an individual to see his or her e-mail address in the "To" line three times. So be sure you follow these instructions:

To: Choose one of the three
BCC: Yourself
BCC: The other two e-mail addresses

Usually if you use this method, the individual you e-mailed doesn't know you have sent it to three addresses in hopes of finding one that works. The failed addresses will simply bounce back and the individual you are sending the e-mail to won't be any the wiser. In the body of the e-mail message, leave no indication that you weren't certain of the address.

Preparing Documents for Fast Submission

Sometimes, bureaucracy won't interfere with the online process and you will be amazed at how fast a department chair or dean responds because he or she is looking for someone with your expertise to teach a class quickly. This is a great position for the online adjunct to be in and you don't want to hold up the process or be a roadblock.

Also remember that, since you will be teaching online, you will need to check your e-mail several times per day. There is no excuse for not doing so; if you are on the road a lot, get a device that allows you to check e-mail. You'll need it once you start teaching, anyway, as you will be required to respond to students and faculty within a certain period of time. Get used to it now! Fast response to the school official or manager shows that you will also be responsive to student needs. Don't let an e-mail sit in the in-box for more than a couple of hours when you start hearing back from individuals at the universities you apply to. Some people will respond immediately and others will take months. Be sure to follow up with those you haven't heard from within a couple of weeks and keep them on your radar screen for two years.

Have available on your computer (and any computer you travel with) the following documents for immediate e-mailing if needed or requested:

- Electronic copies of *all* of your transcripts, especially the last degree completed.
- The address to make a formal request for official transcripts to be sent from previous universities you have attended (and graduated from).
- Your resume or curriculum vitae—the expanded academic version, not your business version.
- Your cover letter.
- References list—three professional references with name, title, e-mail address, and phone number, and three academic references of colleagues or professors, along with name, title, institution, e-mail address, and phone number. (Remember to give your references a heads-up! No surprises!)
- List of the courses you want to teach at the various colleges or schools along with your reasoning (you should note this to yourself as you're sending e-mails.)

- Your teaching web site address, if you have one. If not, a professional (personal, not work!) site will also help.
- Statement of your teaching philosophy. Of everything you write, this will probably be most difficult. In no more than two paragraphs, outline how and why you teach, and what you bring to the classroom. A sample is included at the end of this chapter.

Sample Documents

Introductory E-mail

Your introduction e-mail, whether to HR or to a direct contact, must reflect your personality, your teaching style, and what you'll bring to the table. In academia, the old rules of business don't apply; your resume and your cover letter are expected to be lengthy but *not wordy*. Content is the key here. It is not recommended you directly copy the ideas below into your own introduction and fill in the blanks; chances are many others will have the same introductory message. However, you can use them as starting points and then modify them to suit your style.

Introductory E-mail: Less Formal with a Referral and Experience, No Specific Courses (Resume Attached)

Hello,

Please allow me to introduce myself; my name is Joe Smith. I am an adjunct faculty specializing in technology management, technical courses, and business courses. I received an e-mail from Dr. Test User regarding an open position with your university.

I have taught online courses using Blackboard and WebCT and have taught in the classroom for over three years. I bring a tremendous amount of technology and management experience into the classroom and enjoy knowing I have made a difference in students' knowledge and contributed to students' professional growth.

I have a PhD in Organizational Leadership and Technology Management and an MBA in Business Administration with a Technology emphasis. My prior experience with both in-class and online courses has taught me to be understanding and respectful of student needs, encourage personal and professional growth and responsibility, foster a sense of community, and focus on students' education. Having both taken courses online and taught them, I have a unique perspective on balancing the benefits of online learning with individual learning styles. The eleven years of professional management experience I bring to the classroom help bring real-life examples and case studies to the studies of management and technology.

I feel that my experience both in the classroom and online as well as my commitment to the education of my students would allow me to make a significant contribution to your program. I am attaching my resume for your review, and would love to discuss with you the opportunities you may have for online teaching and how my skill set and qualifications would enhance your program. I may be reached at (999) 555-1212 anytime, or by e-mail at joesmith@myemailaddress.com.

Thank you for your consideration and your time.

Sincerely,

Joe Smith, PhD, MBA, BS

[Signature]

Joe Smith, PhD, MBA
Adjunct Faculty
E-mail: joesmith@myemailaddress.com
Alternative e-mail: joesmith@hotmail.com
Web site: http://www.mywebsite.com
Voice messages (leave e-mail address): 949 555-1212
Cell: (999) 555-1212
Instant Messenger: joesmith@hotmail.com

Note how the multiple contact methods in the signature show how flexible you will be with your students. You are listing a cell phone, a voice mail, a web site, and even an instant messaging address.

Introductory E-mail: Less Formal with a Contact and Experience (Resume Attached)

Dr. Department Chair:

Please allow me to introduce myself; my name is Joe Smith. I am an adjunct faculty specializing in technology management, technical courses, and business courses. I have taught online using Blackboard, WebCT, and numerous other systems, and have taught in the classroom for over three years. I bring a tremendous amount of technology and management experience into the classroom and enjoy knowing I have made a difference in students' knowledge and contributed to students' professional growth.

I was reviewing your web site, which noted the request for IT faculty for the Master's program. Not only did this appear like an exceptional fit, but I have colleagues working at your university who speak very highly of your programs, including Dr. NewJob and Dr. Online, who would provide you with the highest of recommendations regarding my work, work ethic, and experience.

I have a PhD in Organizational Leadership and Technology Management and an MBA in Business Administration with a Technology emphasis. My prior experience with both in-class and online courses has taught me to be understanding and respectful of student needs unique in the online environment, encourage personal and professional growth and responsibility, foster a sense of community, and focus on students' education. Having both taken courses online and taught them, I have a unique perspective on balancing the benefits of online learning with individual learning styles. The years of professional management experience I bring to the classroom help bring real-life examples and case studies to the studies of management and technology. I have also been an IT professional for thirteen years, holding positions such as a Senior IT Director and currently an IT consultant running my own business.

I feel that my experience both in the classroom and online as well as my commitment to the education of my students would allow me to make a significant contribution to your program. I am attaching my resume for your review, and would love to discuss with you the opportunities you may have for online teaching and how my skill set and qualifications would enhance your program. I also have a web site at the address listed below so you may get to know me a bit better. I may be reached at (999) 555-1212 anytime, or by e-mail at joesmith@myemailaddress.com.

Thank you for your consideration and your time.

Sincerely,

Joe Smith, PhD, MBA, BS
[Signature]
Joe Smith, PhD, MBA
Adjunct Faculty
E-mail: joesmith@myemailaddress.com
Alternative e-mail: joesmith@hotmail.com
Web site: http://www.mywebsite.com
Voice messages (leave e-mail address): (949) 555-1212
Cell: (999) 555-1212
Instant Messenger: joesmith@hotmail.com

Address the person you want to work for as "Dear Dr." Use "Dear Human Resources" in your generic HR e-mails. However, when you CC the human resources department, you should address your e-mails to the person you'd be working for along with CC-ing the school dean.

Introductory E-mail: On-Ground Experience, Responding to a Request (Resume Attached)

Dear Dr. XYZ:

This is in reply to your advertisement for Professor of Business Administration/Economics in the *Chronicle of Higher Education*. As the following comparison shows, my experience and background match your requirements.

Your Requirements	My Qualifications
Doctorate in Business Administration	Doctorate in Business Administration from ABC University with a Management emphasis

Commitment to undergraduate teaching	Eleven years' adjunct teaching experience at undergraduate level in eight different colleges; history of exceptional student evaluations
Command of MS Office and statistical software	Five years experience with SAS and SPSS in support of business responsibilities and dissertation analysis; primarily used MS Office since its inception

My adjunct teaching experience includes 24 semesters of statistics, 5 semesters of operations management, 1 semester of marketing research, and an upcoming semester of management science.

My graduate-level education includes over 21 semester hours of statistics/research courses, over 10 hours of economics, and over 11 hours of marketing.

I have enclosed my resume, unofficial transcripts, statement of teaching philosophy, three letters of reference, and student evaluations from several courses I have taught. If you need further information, please call me at (999) 555-1212. I look forward to meeting you.

Yours sincerely,

Joe Smith

Introductory E-mail: Experience, Blind Introductory Letter, with Specific Courses

Dear Human Resources

I am interested in pursuing an adjunct teaching opportunity with the [University] School of [Insert School]. I have a Doctorate in Business Administration from [University]. I also have over 17 years' teaching experience, including dozens of online courses in the past five years. My courses have been at all levels from Associate to Doctorate. Additionally, I have developed numerous courses and served as course director for many.

I would be most interested in teaching [Course Number and Name], [Course Number and Name], [Course Number and Name], and [Course Number and Name]. As you can see from my attached resume, I have significant teaching experience in each of these subjects and have sufficient graduate credits to qualify for teaching them. I even have work experience in these subject areas, which contributes greatly to my ability to teach effectively with adult learners.

I have also attached copies of my transcript so you can preview my qualifications (I will send official transcripts upon request). I am confident I can be a valued asset to your program. I look forward to your reply.

Sincerely,

[Insert graphic of your signature if you have one]

Dr. Joe Smith

Introductory E-mail: Limited Experience, Blind Introductory Letter, No Specific Courses

To Whom It May Concern,

I would like to express my interest in joining [University] as a member of your esteemed faculty. As you will note from my resume, I am currently working on my doctoral degree in [Subject] at [University], an online institution, with a planned completion date of June 2006. I received my graduate degree in Management Information Systems and my undergraduate degree in International Business, both from [University].

I have over 17 years of professional experience, much of which was acquired at Fortune 1000 companies. I have always been directly involved with the business lines of the organizations I have worked for, allowing me to gain a thorough understanding of their primary functional areas. As a project manager, I have either led or been instrumental in seeing many business initiatives come to fruition. [Note how the writer here doesn't have much teaching experience, so he talks about his professional experience and how this will help him in the class-room. This is a very effective method!]

Although my entry into the field of instruction occurred relatively re-cently, I have already espoused the values and practices that I believe are necessary to provide learners with the proper framework to in-crease their self-worth and their value as members of the greater work-force. As an instructor, I place the student, never the material, at the center of my instructional model. I try not to "teach" in the traditional sense of the word, but to facilitate learning, which I believe is a process that begins and ends with the student.

I am a strong believer in the student-centered instructional model. The importance that I place on substantive critical feedback, especially within the online environment, has allowed me to achieve success as an instructor early on, which I always measure in my ability to bring students closer to their individual academic and professional goals, whatever they may be.

I believe that my education and extensive work experience, both as a practitioner and an educator, make me an ideal candidate to join a prestigious institution like [University]. Please contact me at your earli-est convenience so that we may discuss my qualifications in greater detail, as well as the opportunity for me to become an integral part of [University].

Kind regards,

Joe Smith

Curriculum Vitae and Resume

The next thing to focus on is your curriculum vitae (CV), which is essentially a resume that is targeted for academic positions. According to the Capella University Career Center, which provides an incredible service for Capella students and alumni, a CV "is a comprehensive document that emphasizes your education, professional qualifications, and related activities. Effective vitae provide the depth necessary to showcase your qualifications without providing so much information that it overloads the reader. In general, CVs are longer than resumes, and are often two or more pages in length. They are written without using the words 'I,' 'me,' or 'my'" (www.capella.edu).

The Capella University Career Center also advises that your CV focus mainly on your teaching and training experiences. Even if you lack formal experience as an instructor, there are highly transferable skills that you can emphasize, such as training colleagues on new material, presenting at a conference, developing training materials in your job, or providing tutoring or mentoring as a volunteer. Think hard about professional opportunities where you have given a seminar to professionals in a brown bag lunch or in a more formal setting. If this doesn't apply to you, you will need to be sure your introductory e-mail or cover letter reflects how you are starting out in teaching but are bringing your professional experience to the classroom, and that you are looking to change careers for a reason you state. This doesn't eliminate you; we have all started somewhere with no teaching experience. Once you get one or two teaching stints under your belt, you will have the experience to list, and you need to update your resume every single time something changes, including dates, programs, classes, or professional training.

Unlike a resume, which has rather standard sections, a CV allows the significant freedom for you to choose headings that work best for you. The most common sections used are: Education, Certifications, Honors/Awards, Grants/Fellowships Received, Publications, Institutional Service/Committee Work, Languages, Computer/Technical Skills, Teaching and Training Experience, Related Professional Experience, Internships/Assistantships, Professional Memberships/Associations, Presentations Given, Community Involvement/Volunteer Activities, Specialized Training Received, and Professional Development. The Capella University Career Center advises that experience and activities within each section be listed in reverse chronological order.

The Capella University Career Center also advises that you emphasize the impact of your work on your organizations with bullet points and action words. Here are some examples taken directly from the Capella web site:

- Trained 18 new clerical staff, resulting in standardized application of procedures and improved customer satisfaction.
- Introduced Business and Accounting Department to online teaching platform technology leading to the delivery of three courses online.
- Created new procedure for escalating customer complaints, resulting in increased customer satisfaction and significant repeat business.
- Taught two-day job transition seminars increasing participants' knowledge of career management and job search strategies.

From personal experience, we recommend that you be aware that if you already work for numerous schools, some of them may be concerned you might be overworked and won't be able to dedicate yourself to their programs. In such a case, you may want to consider removing those that don't take up much of your time but clutter up your resume. Experience is important, but the university that is hiring you also wants some degree of commitment and may not appreciate your being a professional adjunct, even if you are excellent at what you do for every university.

The following sample resumes of Joseph A. Smith and Rachelle S. Johnston were provided by Amy Olmscheid and Julie Ofstedal of the Capella University Career Center. You will notice that there is no executive summary at the top, as Amy doesn't recommend them for academic CVs (but does recommend them for corporate resumes); she recommends that you include the summary information in your cover letter instead. Also included is a modified resume for Dr. Jim Mirabella.

[While the schools used in the resume are real, the person is fictional. Any resemblance to real persons, living or dead, is purely coincidental.]

Joseph A. Smith
222 South 9th Street • Minneapolis, MN 55402
612.555.5000 • joesmith@myemail.com

EDUCATION

PhD, Organization and Management

Capella University, Minneapolis, MN   Expected 2007

Specialization: **Human Resource Management**

Dissertation: *Improving the Modeling and Measurement of Personality Assessments Used for Hiring Decisions at Fortune 500 Companies*

MBA

University of St. Thomas, St. Paul, MN   2003

BA, Business/Human Resource Management

Metropolitan State University, Minneapolis, MN   1989

TEACHING & TRAINING EXPERIENCE

Adjunct Instructor   2004–present

Minneapolis Community and Technical College, Minneapolis, Minnesota

Courses taught: *Introduction to Business, Principles of Management*

- Taught 12-week courses to diverse adult populations.
- Developed study guides, weekly quizzes, and final examinations.

Instructor   2002–2003

Larson Hilman, Bloomington, Minnesota

- Taught two-day *Managing Your Search Project* seminar to adults in job transition. Units included: surveying professional environment, determining a professional objective, creating communications strategy and resume, creating an effective job search strategy, defining target market, networking, interviewing, and negotiation.
- Received consistently high student evaluation marks (4.5+ on 5.0 scale).

PROFESSIONAL EXPERIENCE

Thrivent Financial, Minneapolis, MN

Human Resource Administrator, Insurance Division   2003–Present

- Supervise and provide payroll and human resource consulting for 175 employees in three states.

- Develop administrative office policies and procedures to streamline office operations.
- Collaborate with department managers and directors to develop employee retention initiatives resulting in less employee turnover and significant cost savings.
- Update job descriptions, performance standards, midyear evaluations in human resource employee records with 98% accuracy.
- Write annual and midyear performance reviews and narratives for awards.
- Cross-train administrative employees and new hires to provide career development opportunities and backup skills resulting in 95% accuracy on audit reports and other administrative operations.
- Monitor submission of performance appraisals, promotions for all employees.

Deluxe Corporation, Shoreview, MN
Human Resource Generalist   2000–2003
- Served as a liaison between the hiring managers and employment agencies by screening agency candidates and conducting interviews.
- Oversaw the pre-employment screening process including applicant references, criminal checks, bondability and drug testing.
- Created an employee evaluation plan, resulting in improved evaluation efficiency.
- Supervised maintenance of job postings on company web site, ensuring accurate dissemination of open positions.
- Advertised job openings to internal candidates, and managed their applications.
- Managed the administration of the Harrison Inner View, and all other pre-employment tests.

PRESENTATIONS
Creating Effective HR Strategies, presented to 50+ participants at the Society for Human Resource Management's Strategic HR Conference, Washington, DC, 2005.

The Use of Personality Assessments in Hiring Decisions, presented at Career Planning and Adult Development (CPAD) monthly meeting, St. Paul, MN, 2005.

Negotiation Skills for the HR Professional, presented at the Capella University Residential Colloquium, Scottsdale, AZ, 2004.

Quality Tools and Methods for Measuring Performance, presented at Twin Cities Human Resource Association Annual Conference, Minneapolis, MN, 2002.

PUBLICATIONS

Smith, J. A. (2004). "IT Outsourcing and Offshoring." *NACE Web* Magazine. www.careerperformancestrategies.com.

PROFESSIONAL ASSOCIATIONS

Society of Human Resource Management (SHRM)	2001–Present
National Association of Colleges and Employers	2004–Present
Twin Cities Human Resource Society	2004–Present

- <u>Membership Chair</u>, 2005–Present

GRANTS

Minnesota WGC Foundation: Carol M. Olson Program Grant   2004
- Co-authored grant for Neighborhood Involvement Program, received $6,000 to develop employment program for inner-city youth.

INSTITUTIONAL SERVICE

Minneapolis Community and Technical College,   2005–Present
Minneapolis, MN
<u>Committee Member, New Hire Training Commission</u>

VOLUNTEER EXPERIENCE

- Volunteer Counselor, Neighborhood Involvement   2002–Present
  Programs, Minneapolis, MN
- HealthyLiving Minnesota Speaker's Bureau   Educator, 1992–Present
  Minneapolis, MN

OTHER WORK HISTORY

St. Paul Fire & Marine Insurance Co., St. Paul, MN

Regional Manager	1998–2000
Sr. Project Leader	1997–1998
Sr. Field Technology Analyst	1996–1997
Help Desk Analyst	1994–1996
Database Administrator, Software Instructor, LAN	1987–1994
Software Testing Supervisor	

[While the schools used in the resume are real, the person is fictional. Any resemblance to real persons, living or dead, is purely coincidental.]

Rachelle S. Johnston
862 Zero Street • North Platte, NE 69101
(308) 555-8905 • rachellejohnston@email.net

EDUCATION

PhD in Education	In progress, expected 2008
Capella University, Minneapolis MN	
Master of Education	2004
University of Nebraska, Lincoln, NE	
Bachelor of Arts in Elementary Education	1994
Texas Tech University, Lubbock, TX	

CURRENT TEACHING CERTIFICATIONS

Reading Specialist in Nebraska, K–12	2000
Elementary Education in Nebraska, K–9	1999

HIGHER EDUCATION TEACHING EXPERIENCE

Instructor   2006–Present
Area Community College, Lincoln, NE

- Teach **Foundations of Education** to undergraduate students both online and in person.

Developed discussion questions, quizzes, and examinations to assess learning outcomes.

TEACHING EXPERIENCE

Title I Reading Specialist/ESL Instructor   2003–Present
Adams Middle School, North Platte, NE

- Teach curriculum aligned with district guidelines to 25+ students.
- Instruct students using research-based reading strategies.
- Train staff members on implementation of reading assessments.
- Provide support to non-English-speaking students in the classroom.

Fourth Grade Teacher   1999–2001
West Lincoln Elementary School, Lincoln, NE

- Provided instruction in all academic areas to students in grade 4.
- Designed and implemented a new reading program that raised reading scores 20% on average.
- Piloted and trained teachers on new computerized report card.
- Developed a remedial reading program for West Lincoln Elementary School.

Second Grade Teacher/Special Education Teacher
Eastridge Elementary School, Lincoln, NE   1997–1999

- Implemented learning strategies for children with special needs.
- Established effective communication among students, teachers and parents between home and school.

- Served on districtwide committees, including the Data Collection, Superintendent Selection, and School Improvement committees.

RELATED EXPERIENCE

Peer Tutor and Freshman Mentor
Texas Tech University, Lubbock, TX   1995–1997
- Served as a writing tutor to undergraduate students.
- Provided leadership and guidance to freshman undergraduate students.
- Taught College Survival course to incoming freshman students.

PRESENTATIONS GIVEN

Johnston, R. S., & Samson, D. (March 2003). *Differentiated Teaching Strategies in the K–12 English Classroom.* Presented at the National Reading Conference, Newark, NJ.

Johnston, R. S. (August 2003). *Preparing Children for Reading Testing.* Workshop presented at the 2nd Annual Nebraska Reading and Learning Conference, Lincoln, NE.

Johnston, R. S. (October 2002). *Strategies for Success: Integrating Technology into Reading Curriculum.* Workshop presented to the semiannual meeting of the Dallas Reading Council, Dallas, TX.

Johnston, R. S. (September 2000). *Reading and Writing in the Special Needs Classroom.* Workshop presented to the semiannual meeting of the Dallas Reading Council, Dallas, TX.

Johnston, R. S., & Vick, T. (April 1998). *Teaching Practical Learning Skills to Children with Special Needs.* Paper presented at the nineteenth annual conference of the Texas Association of Developmental Education, Lubbock, TX.

COMMUNITY SERVICE

School Board Member   2003–Present
Adams Middle School, North Platte, NE

Curriculum Committee Member   2002–Present
Adams Middle School, North Platte, NE

Lincoln County Youth Association Volunteer   2001– Present
- Volunteer mentor and event planner

AWARDS

Teacher of the Year Nomination   2001
West Lincoln Elementary School, Lincoln, NE

PROFESSIONAL MEMBERSHIPS

National Education Association   2003–Present
Nebraska State Education Association   2000–Present
Nebraska Council of Teachers of English   1999–Present

James W. Mirabella
123 XYZ Street • Jacksonville, Florida
drjim@email.com • (904) 555-5555

EDUCATION

Doctorate in Business Administration, specialization in **Management**
Nova SouthEastern University, Ft. Lauderdale, FL   1999
Dissertation: *Employee Preferences for Pay Systems as a Function of Personal Job Inputs and Job Characteristics*
Master's in Business Administration
Auburn University, Montgomery, AL   1988
Master's in Statistics (12 sem. hrs. completed)
University of North Florida, Jacksonville, FL   1996
Bachelor of Science, Operations Research & Statistics
U.S. Air Force Academy, CO   1985

TEACHING AND TRAINING EXPERIENCE

Capella University, Minneapolis, MN   2002–Present
Adjunct professor of online PhD courses in: *Statistics, Research Methods, Survey Design*
- Lead faculty for online Statistics courses.
- Developed two online PhD courses in Statistics and one online MS course in Statistics.
- Mentored 10 students to completion of their PhD.
- Served as research methodologist for 17 PhD committees.

___ **University**, City, State   1998–Present
Adjunct professor of BS & MBA courses in: *Statistics, Quantitative Analysis, Operations Management*
- Developed hybrid courses in Statistics and Quantitative Analysis

___ **University**, Jacksonville, FL   1995–Present
Adjunct professor of MBA/MA courses in: *Statistics, Research Methods, Operations Management*
- Faculty chair for MBA in Jacksonville campus
- Developed online MBA course in Statistics

___ **University**, City, State   2004–Present
Adjunct professor of online PhD courses in: *Statistics, Research, Management*
- Faculty chair for Doctoral Research in School of Education.
- Faculty chair for Quantitative Methods in School of Business.
- Developed online courses in Statistics for the Schools of Business and Education.

___ **College**, City, STATE   1996–Present
Adjunct professor of AA-level courses in: *Statistics*
• Developed hybrid course in Statistics.
___ **University**, City, STATE   2003– Present
Adjunct professor of online Master's-level courses in: *Operations Management, Marketing Research*
___ **University**, City, State   2004–Present
Adjunct professor of online Master's-level courses in: *Statistics*
• Developed online course in Statistics.
• Quality auditor and quality coach for Master's program.
___ **College**, City, State   2003– 2005
Adjunct professor of online Master's-level courses in: *Statistics*
___ **University**, City, State   1998–2005
Adjunct professor of online PhD-level courses in: *Research Methods*
Adjunct professor of BS & Master's-level courses in: *Statistics, Operations Management*
___ **University**, City, State   1991–1996
Adjunct professor of BS-level courses in: *Statistics, Calculus, Algebra*
___ **University**, City, State   1988–1990
Adjunct professor of BS-level courses in: *Statistics*

COLLEGE-LEVEL COURSES TAUGHT (AS OF SPRING 2006)

COURSE	LEVEL	# TIMES TAUGHT
Statistics (*online*)	Doctorate	48
Research Methods (*online*)	Doctorate	26
Research Methods	Doctorate	7
Operations Management	Doctorate	3
Dissertation Research	Doctorate	5
Survey Research Methods (*online*)	Doctorate	1
Total Quality Management (*online*)	Doctorate	1
Business & Management (*online*)	Doctorate	2
Statistics (*online*)	Master's	30
Statistics	Master's	23
Operations Management	Master's	19
Research & Assessment	Master's	17
Quantitative Analysis	Master's	5
Marketing Research	Master's	4
Operations Management (*online*)	Master's	1
Quantitative Analysis (*online*)	Master's	1
Compensation Management	Master's	1

Statistics	Undergraduate	74
Quantitative Analysis	Undergraduate	16
College Algebra	Undergraduate	5
Operations Management	Undergraduate	4
Calculus	Undergraduate	2

RELATED ACCOMPLISHMENTS

Statistical Analysis/Research

- Analyzed employee survey responses for a large, local hospital as well as the Chamber of Commerce. Also helped with the design of the survey.
- Conducted educational research on (1) the optimal class size for student success, (2) the comparative success of students registering late vs. on time, (3) student success as a function of college readiness, (4) online success, (5) scheduling courses for optimal success, and (6) modeling for student retention.
- Used multiple regression to forecast student enrollments for three years with less than 1% error.
- Used SPSS CHAID analysis at a call center to reduce outbound sales calls by 50% while capturing over 75% of the potential sales. This increased sales by over 50%.
- Modeled corporate measurements to predict client satisfaction results, with a correlation of 0.92.
- Used SAS statistical tests, locating a three-year error in a demographic database, recovering $200K.
- Programmed, designed, and implemented simulation and trend analysis models for Air Force Quality Assurance and reduced required man-hours by 60%.
- Analyzed Perrier inbound sales activity vs. advertising to accurately predict call volumes following each ad; used the results to advise Perrier on when to advertise and on the best use of advertising media.
- Designed a statistical experiment for evaluating two simultaneous innovations in improving call handling time; the study looked at cost effectiveness and learning curves while focusing on client satisfaction.
- Designed a customer satisfaction survey to measure the value our call center added to a client. Despite lower-priced competitors, our results garnered a contract extension.

TOTAL QUALITY MANAGEMENT/EDUCATIONAL LEADERSHIP/CORPORATE LEADERSHIP

- Consulted over 20 Process Management Teams in the selection of goals, the development of metrics, the collecting and reporting of data, the follow-up root cause analysis, and the use of *Six Sigma*.
- Participated as a Quality Award examiner for two years, and organization won Malcolm Baldrige Award.
- Led the campus deans and other personnel on a Data Integrity team at Florida Community College, with the purpose of improving student records reported to the state; this resulted in thousands of students graduating after being previously overlooked, as well as increased funding for the school.
- Built a team of research analysts and programmers to streamline college's Institutional Research.
- Led a Quality organization, supporting the Customer Satisfaction, Employee Recognition, and Benchmarking teams.
- Implemented several best practices on call center accounts, reducing turnover and improving client satisfaction on the accounts, and attaining a best-in-class certification in a TARP benchmarking study.

WORK HISTORY

Mirabella Research Services, Inc., Jacksonville, FL   2002–Present

President

Responsible for consulting and training in survey design, research and statistical analysis.

Florida Community College. Jacksonville, FL   1999–2002

Director of Institutional Research

Responsible for conducting ad hoc research, survey design and analysis, and report writing. Also responsible for validating the integrity of student/faculty data, submitting the data and reports to the Department of Education, and corresponding with members of the DOE as well as the college leaders.

Convergys Corporation (formerly AT&T), Jacksonville, FL   1996–1999

Director of Quality and Recognition

Responsible for leading the Quality and Recognition team; this includes designing, implementing, and analyzing employee and client surveys, as well as designing and evaluating corporate measurements. Also responsible for working with various process teams to improve quality via statistical quality control tools.

AT&T American Transtech, Jacksonville, FL   1994–1996

Marketing Research Statistical Analyst

Responsible for conducting demographic analysis on customers who contacted the various call center accounts so as to provide clients with valuable marketing data. Also responsible for conducting target marketing analysis (on request) to include the use of CHAID.

AT&T, Oakton, VA, and Conyers, GA   1990–1994

Statistical Quality Control Consultant/ISO Internal Quality Auditor

Responsible for consulting with goals, metrics, data collection/reports, and follow-up root cause analysis. Served as an internal quality auditor to prepare for ISO 9001 registration and the Malcolm Baldrige Award.

U.S. Air Force, Montgomery, AL   June 1985–May 1990

Operations Research Analyst/Captain, U.S.A.F.

Responsible for database programming, simulation modeling, and trend analysis modeling for the U.S. Air Force. The position involved writing/testing programs for almost every Air Force Command.

PROFESSIONAL PRESENTATIONS GIVEN

WORKSHOP TITLE	ORGANIZATIONS
Hypothesis Testing with SPSS	➤ Capella University Colloquia, 2006
Statistical Thinking	➤ Capella University Colloquia, 2004–2006
	➤ Florida Sterling Conference, 1998
	➤ Project Management Institute, 1997
	➤ American Society for Quality, 1998
Sampling for Surveys	➤ Capella University Colloquia, 2003–2006
	➤ Florida Sterling Conference, 2000, 2003
How Not to Write a Survey	➤ Capella University Colloquia, 2003–2006
SPSS for Beginners	➤ Capella University Colloquia, 2004–2005
Mapping Out a Quantitative Study	➤ Capella University Colloquia, 2004–2006
Continuous Quality Improvement	➤ Capella University Colloquia, 2005
Six Sigma for Beginners	➤ Bombardier Capital, 2000
Statistical Toolbox	➤ Florida Sterling Conference, 1997
	➤ Jacksonville Quality Exchange, 1996

Using Surveys to Measure Customer Satisfaction

Statistics 101—Misuses of Statistics

What Gets Measured Gets Undone

Research for Measurement and Analysis

➢ Florida Sterling Conference, 1998
➢ Amelia Island Plantation, 1999
➢ Florida Sterling Conference, 1999–2001
➢ Florida Sterling Conference, 2000–2001
➢ Florida Sterling Conference, 2001
➢ American Society for Quality, 2002

PROFESSIONAL PUBLICATIONS

Mirabella, J. (2006). *Hypothesis Testing with SPSS: A Non-Statistician's Guide & Tutorial*. Companion resource manual for Capella University Colloquia.

Mirabella, J. (2006). *SPSS: A Live Demo*. Companion resource manual for Capella University Colloquia.

Mirabella, J., Babb, D., & Lazo, A. (2006). "Factors Driving Employee Pay Criterion in Corporations." *International Management Review Journal* (1).

Green, K., Broome, H., and Mirabella, J. (2006). "Postnatal Depression in Arabic Mothers: Socio-Cultural and Physical Factors. *Journal of Psychology, Health and Medicine*, publication date TBD.

Loescher, K., Hughes, R., Cavico, F., Mirabella, J., and Pellet, P. (2005) "The Impact of an 'Ethics Across the Curriculum' Initiative on the Cognitive Moral Development of Business School Undergraduates." *Teaching Ethics*, 5(2) 31.

Mirabella, J. (2001) *Plugging the Leaking Bucket of First Year Dropouts*. Paper presented at the 2001 Southeastern Association of Community College Research Conference in August, 2001.

PROFESSIONAL MEMBERSHIPS

Decision Sciences Institute	2004–Present
American Society for Quality (ASQ Certified Quality Engineer since 2000)	1991–Present
Association of Collegiate Business Schools and Programs	2005–Present

COMPUTER/TECHNICAL SKILLS

¬ Statistical Analysis

➢ Blackboard & WebCT

➢ E-College

➢ Survey Design & Analysis

➢ SPSS Statistical Software

➢ MicroSoft Excel

➢ Research Methodologies

➢ SAS Statistical Software

➢ Database Marketing

Sample Resume: With Teaching Experience, Professional Experience, and Degrees

JANE JONES, PHD, MBA, BS
2000 Online School Drive, Best City, FL 77887
Voice Messages: (949) 555-1212 ; Mobile: (999) 555-1212
E-Mail or Instant Messenger: janejones@myemail.com

SUMMARY

Energetic and educated professional with teaching experience in Information Technology and Business courses, I have over twelve years management experience in business and healthcare IT. My learner-focused attitude and best practice teaching methods enable students to gain a real-world understanding of theory and principles. Excellent social skills help encourage approachability and foster a comfortable learning environment both online and in the classroom. A professional mentor and coach, I have successfully served students in numerous capacities, including faculty mentor, dissertation committee member, and comprehensive examination committee member. I have a solid background and firm understanding of the process required to develop program objectives and map course curriculum to achieve desired student outcomes, and have put this into practice as a course developer and review committee member.

PERSONAL ATTRIBUTES

Educated in Business and Technology; well versed in the application of business objectives to technology principles and their application to business and healthcare.

Highly competent, outcomes driven with exceptional organizational skills.

Extraordinarily responsive, attentive, and precise communication with students and peers.

Excellent references and recommendations by Department Chairs, students, and colleagues.

Experienced in online and in-classroom courses, I understand difficulties that the online environment can bring and have applied workable solutions to these issues.

Real-life current management experience in Information Technology within several industries including health care, manufacturing, real estate, and construction.

Proactive; concerned with student education, understanding and responsive to the balance of student needs with department needs.

Sample Documents

PROFESSIONAL ACCOMPLISHMENTS

Faculty or Course Development Positions (some courses may be taught only one time per year)

[School Name], Adjunct Faculty　　　　　　**March 2004 to present**
Bachelor's and Master's in Business

Courses taught in Blackboard:

[Course Number—Course Name (online or on-ground)
Put information here about the course. Include the level it was taught at, and if appropriate, the course description from the catalog. Be sure this is very accurate information.]

[School Name], Adjunct Faculty　　　　　　**March 2001 to present**
Master's and Doctoral Degrees in Management
Dissertation and Comprehensive Examination Committees

Courses taught in WebCT and Lotus:

[Course Number—Course Name (online or on-ground)
Put information here about the course. Include the level it was taught at and, if appropriate, the course description from the catalog. Be sure this is very accurate information. Also note if you revised or developed the course and, if it's online, which platform it was taught in.]

Courses taught in Blackboard:

[Course Number—Course Name (online or on-ground)
Put information here about the course. Include the level it was taught at and, if appropriate, the course description from the catalog. Be sure this is very accurate information. Also note if you revised or developed the course and, if it's online, which platform it was taught in.]

[School Name], Adjunct Faculty (online)　　　　**April 2002 to present**
Bachelor's in Business
Dissertation and Comprehensive Examination Committees

Courses taught in Blackboard:

[Course Number—Course Name (online or on-ground)
Put information here about the course. Include the level it was taught at and, if appropriate, the course description from the catalog. Be sure this is very accurate information. Also note if you revised or developed the course and, if it's online, which platform it was taught in.]

[School Name], Adjunct Faculty (online)   **April 2004 to present**
Bachelor's in Business
Dissertation and Comprehensive Examination Committees

Courses taught in Blackboard:

Courses taught in online digital drop box system:

[Course Number—Course Name (online or on-ground)
Put information here about the course. Include the level it was taught at and, if appropriate, the course description from the catalog. Be sure this is very accurate information. Also note if you revised or developed the course and, if it's online, which platform it was taught in.
Course development for the above course.]

[School Name], Adjunct Faculty (online)   **April 2004 to present**
Bachelor's in Business
Dissertation and Comprehensive Examination Committees

Courses taught in Blackboard:

Courses taught on-ground:

[Course Number—Course Name
Put information here about the course. Include the level it was taught at and, if appropriate, the course description from the catalog. Be sure this is very accurate information. Also note if you revised or developed the course and, if it's online, which platform it was taught in.]

Previous Educator/Course Developer/Teaching Positions

University of Whatever School, Online Instructor   August 2003 to March 2005
Bachelor's and Master's Information Technology Programs

Courses taught:

[Course Name
Put information here about the course. Include the level it was taught at and, if appropriate, the course description from the catalog. Be sure this is very accurate information. Also note if you revised or developed the course and, if it's online, which platform it was taught in.]

Courses developed:

[Course Name
Put information here about the course. Include the level it was taught at and, if appropriate, the course description from the catalog. Be sure this is very accurate information. Also note if you revised or developed the course and, if it's online, which platform it was taught in.]

[University, School]
Adjunct Faculty—September 1999 to December 2002
Master's of Health Information Systems Program

[University, School]
Assistant Professor—September 1999 to June 2001
Master's of Health Information Systems Program

Courses taught:

[Course Name
Put information here about the course. Include the level it was taught at and, if appropriate, the course description from the catalog. Be sure this is very accurate information. Also note if you revised or developed the course and, if it's online, which platform it was taught in.]

Management Positions

[Company], Newport Beach, CA   March 2004 to November 2005
[Put a description of what the company did here.]

Title
[Note what you were responsible for followed by details below.

Item 1 that you did, along with deliverables, and how this experience will help you in the classroom.

Item 2 that you did, along with deliverables, and how this experience will help you in the classroom.]

[Company], Newport Beach, CA   March 2001 to November 2003
[Put a description of what the company did here.]

Title
[Note what you were responsible for followed by details below.

Item 1 that you did, along with deliverables, and how this experience will help you in the classroom.

Item 2 that you did, along with deliverables, and how this experience will help you in the classroom.

Go back to all of your previous positions, minus items like "burger joint chef."]

Technical Positions

[Company

Title   **July 1992 to July 1994**
Other positions you held there]

Entrepreneurial Experience

Owner and Founder of [Company Name]   **1996–2001**

Owned and operated IT consulting business acting as an outsourced IT help desk for small to medium-sized businesses. Currently side business, run by contractors. Business has provided tremendous experience in all aspects of business including marketing, sales, finance, planning, business development, and customer service.

Formal and Professional Education

PhD in [Degree, Emphasis
School, Month, Year. GPA]

Master's in [Degree, Emphasis
School, Month, Year. GPA]

Bachelor of [Degree, Emphasis
School, Month, Year. GPA]

[Training title, year]

[Seminar, year]

[List online classroom training from various universities and your accomplishments in the training sessions.]

Publications, Research, and Presentations

[These are from one of the authors' publications, research, and presentations section. List these by year, not alphabetically. Ideally these are all yours so you don't need to alphabetize.]

Babb, D. (2005). "Current Developments and Trends in IT and Their Impact on the Real Estate Business Sector." *A Review of Literature, Technology and Primary Research*—International Symposium on Computer Science and Technology 2005, Ningbo, China.

Babb, D. (2005). "Factors Influencing Use of Virtual Private Networks over Traditional Wide Area Networks by Decision Making Technology Managers." International Symposium on Computer Science and Technology 2005, Ningbo, China.

Babb, D. (2005). "Factors Influencing Virtual Private Network Adoption Decisions." *Proceedings from 2005 International Symposium on Computer Science and Technology*. American Scholars Press, p. 16. ISBN 0-9721479-5-0.

Babb, D. May (2000). "Determination of Characteristics to Define Users' Perception of Support Using Regression Analysis."

108

Babb, D. (December 1999). "Cost Savings Associated with Virtual Private Networking." Master's thesis.

Highly Competent Subject Areas

Cisco Internetworking, Network Design, Server Administration, Data Communications Theories and Practice, Strategic Management, Computer Network Administration, Computer Hardware, Computer Software, Use of Computers in Organizations, Windows Platforms, TCP/IP and Networking, Project Planning, Analysis, Business and Technology, Strategic Planning, Economics, Statistics, Human Resources (Compensation, Recruiting, Retention), Communication, Health Care Information Systems. [This is an example. List every single thing you're good at; it will be a basis for what you are competent to teach in. Don't put anything here if you aren't qualified to teach it.]

Educational and Management References

[Name], PhD; Professor of Statistics
Adjunct Faculty
E-mail:
Phone:

[Name], PhD; Professor of Statistics
Adjunct Faculty
E-mail:
Phone:

[Name], MBA; Business Systems Analyst
[Company Name]
E-mail:
Phone:

Sample Resume: With Limited Teaching Experience, Professional Experience, and Degrees

Name
Address
Phone, E-mail

Objective:

Seeking a challenging position in academia where I can utilize my work experience and fondness for pedagogy to build upon a career that provides me with the desired scholar-practitioner balance in my life.

109

Education:

01/04–07/06   *Doctor of Philosophy*

[Program (Specialization)]
(ABD: December 2005; Planned completion: June 2006)
[University]
[Note that the applicant here isn't done with his/her doctorate. However, he/she is ABD (all but dissertation). While this isn't a professionally or academically recognized standard or title like PhD or MBA, it is a status in terms of where you are in a program. If you are an ABD student, you should note it like this individual has.]

08/99–01/02   *Master of Science*

[Program (Specialization)
University, School]

08/94–05/98   *Bachelor of Arts*

[Program (Specialization)
University, School]

Work Experience:

06/05–Present   *[University—Faculty]*
Currently teaching [Course Number (Course Name) and Course Number (Course Name).]
Also approved to teach the following courses:
[Course Number (Course Name)
Course Number (Course Name)
Course Number (Course Name)
Course Number (Course Name)]

08/99–Present   *[Company—Title]*
[Discuss in detail what you actually do for this organization. It is acceptable and encouraged to add one sentence regarding how this will help you in the classroom. Be sure to discuss any training that you have given or presentations you've made.]

Achievements Include:
• [List specific, measurable achievements.]

08/93–07/99   *[Company—Title]*
[Discuss in detail what you actually did for this organization. It is acceptable and encouraged to add one sentence regarding how this will help you in the

classroom. be sure to discuss any training that you have given or presentations you've made.]

Achievements Include:
• [List specific, measurable achievements.]

Other Teaching Experience:

02/05–Present   *[University]—Guest Lecturer*

Statement of Teaching Philosophy

It is imperative that you think about this a lot; write down adjectives that describe you and verbs that describe your style, and put your philosophy into not more than two paragraphs. This tells the university what kind of teacher you are and the philosophies you subscribe to, and will help the administrators determine whether you are a good match for the university.

As I see it, a teacher serves the needs of his/her customers—the students. Each student pays for and is entitled to the best education possible. A teacher should have a passion for his/her subject and should be capable of taking different instructional approaches for the diverse learning styles of students. Teachers serve not only to instruct but also to facilitate discussion among the students. Each student has something valuable to bring into a classroom, and a teacher should be capable of gleaning that collective knowledge and experience.

The role of a teacher extends beyond the classroom. He/she not only is to educate students on the material, but also to serve as a compass, giving the student direction and guidance, and essentially helping to develop the whole student with an emphasis on leadership. A teacher serves as one of the greatest role models, and is the students' link to the business world. It is only with knowledgeable, dedicated teachers that a student is positioned for success.

Statement of Online Teaching Philosophy (May Be Used as a Philosophy Statement)

Online distance learning has opened new educational doors like nothing before in history. It has afforded the opportunity for individuals who may not have otherwise had an opportunity to further their education, due to professional or personal constraints, and allows them to do so in an environment that is facilitative and conducive to their success. Online delivery is a unique blend of creating a warm and inviting environment, encouragement by untraditional means (e-mail, phone calls if needed, instant messaging), and the ability to provide first-rate service to students without being in the same room. Online facilitators must be available and understand that most students have strong professional or personal history and desire respect for this experience. They need a place where theory and their experiences can be blended together, which will encourage their knowledge, growth, and understanding of topics important in today's marketplace.

Sample of E-Mail to Send as Follow-Up

If you've followed our instructions, you have a folder of e-mails that you need to follow up on either because you have heard nothing or because you were asked to follow up. Here is a short and sweet example of what you may choose to send.

Hi [Name],

My name is Jane Jones; we corresponded some time ago about possible adjunct teaching opportunities either online or on-ground in the

Business and Management Department or IT Department. I wanted to check in with you and see if you were in need of any additional faculty for the upcoming term. I have attached my most recent professional resume.

Best regards,
Jane Jones, PhD

Sample of E-Mail to Send If the University Requests a List of Courses You Want to Teach

Sometimes universities will respond with a request for a list of courses you're interested in teaching. This is why we recommend doing your homework up front and listing your preference in the introductory e-mail. Nonetheless, if you choose to go the generic route, here is a sample of this sort of follow-up e-mail.

Hi [Name],

I've been in contact with [Name] on the [department] courses that I'd like to teach. The remaining courses I'd be interested (and qualified) to teach are:

Business and Management:
[Course Number, Course Name]
[Course Number, Course Name]

Health Care IT:
[Course Number, Course Name]
[Course Number, Course Name]

Management Information Systems (MIS):
[Course Number, Course Name]
[Course Number, Course Name]

HR:
[Course Number, Course Name]

Information Systems:
[Course Number, Course Name]
[Course Number, Course Name]

Thanks, [Name]; I appreciate you forwarding this to the appropriate course managers or chairs.

Best regards,
Jane

7

The Interview: What Universities Look For

In a completely rational society, the best of us would be teachers and the rest of us would have to settle for something less.

—Lee Iacocca

So you have gotten your application to the university and you have piqued their interest. Good for you! This is a critical accomplishment and you should be proud. Now you need to prepare yourself for the more crucial step—closing the deal! As with any job interview, you have to step up and make yourself stand above the rest of the crowd vying for the same position. Sometimes you are lucky and have a niche, one for which the university is badly in need of people with your qualifications. However, if you teach general business courses, you might find yourself competing with people who have more education and/or more experience.

You have now reached the often-dreaded interview process. Relatively speaking, most of these don't compare with business interviews in difficulty level. Very rarely is there an in-person interview; sometimes there isn't even a phone call. While the process of applying for the adjunct positions is similar to the business application process at first, once you get to this stage, you must take it up a notch. Suddenly the script is gone and you are left to sell yourself in a way that varies from university to university. Take solace in knowing that there are some common themes and you will get good at this very quickly, especially if you flood the market with applications as we suggested. Our suggestion to apply for your less desired universities first applies here since you want the practice for what to expect in an interview process before you try for your top choices. In this chapter we look at the interview process, what to expect from it, and how to prepare yourself for it.

Interview Processes of Online Schools

Let us first differentiate interview processes by type of university. Specifically, we examine interview processes for traditional universities, nontraditional universities and community colleges, and faith-based schools.

Traditional universities are the bricks-and-mortar places with live classrooms, a limited enrollment, and a minimum score required on College Board exams; they usually have a real campus with dormitories and sports teams. The nontraditional universities and community colleges typically have unlimited enrollment or what is sometimes referred to as open enrollment, often have no College Board requirements, sometimes offer online courses or are online schools, and often seem to be hiring. The faith-based schools can be partially or completely online and often have open enrollment, but have an interview process that rivals and challenges those of traditional universities and models in many ways.

Traditional Universities

The traditional university that has added an online program has a well-established faculty and a reputation built on selectivity of students. It does not have open enrollment and so can afford to be picky about who teaches

116

there. The more elite universities utilize their full-time faculty in the on-line program to promote the reputation of the online program as equaling the classroom. Job openings are typically advertised in *The Chronicle of Higher Education* (www.chronicle.com).

If you are lucky enough to be selected for an interview with one of these universities, be prepared for an interview process that mirrors what you would do if you were trying to get a full-time job there. You can expect to be sent detailed questionnaires that probe you beyond the standard application. They will want to know about your specific skills, use of Web technology, your teaching philosophy, whether you have published re-cently in any academic journals, as well as some other pertinent and time-consuming information requests. What is asked is unique to each university, but you can expect some common themes; the questions are not too difficult to answer but may take more time than you expected. Note here that your written response is part of the interview. How you re-spond, how quickly you do it, and how professional and well-written it is will carry a lot of weight in whether you advance in the interview process. From the moment you receive anything from the university asking more of you, remind yourself that you are always being graded, so keep your wits about you.

Whether or not you do fill out an interview questionnaire, you can expect a phone interview. In fact, you can expect several phone interviews, beginning with the search committee or department chair or possibly with human resources, and eventually leading up to the dean. Sometimes you will have several people interviewing you at one time, often including full-time tenured professors from that university.

Expect to be asked easy questions like: "Tell us about your online teaching experience," "What courses have you taught online?," "For whom have you taught online?," and "Why do you enjoy teaching online?" Other common questions you may hear are "How is teaching online different from teaching on ground?" and "What exceptions do you make when teaching online compared with your on-ground experience?" (That is as-suming, of course, that you have some experience in both venues.)

After you are comfortable with the interview, expect things to be turned up a notch with "Why do you want to teach for Whatsamatta U.?," "What unique skills do you possess that would benefit Whatsamatta U.?," "What are your strengths and weaknesses as an online professor?," "How does your teaching philosophy fit in with the culture here at Whatsamatta U.?," and (one of our favorites) "We are currently interviewing 18 candidates for this position; why should we hire you?" Imagine trying to answer these impromptu, especially when they tell you that you are allowed only three minutes to answer each question. Don't be surprised when they wrap up the call and ask if you have any questions for them; if you have none, they may see it as a sign that you are not interested and haven't done your homework. It is really important that you've searched the Web, are familiar with the school's programs and reputation, and have a list of questions to ask that show your interest. These should be genuine questions; after all, most likely you do in fact have questions you need answers to. Consider the following as food for thought: "What are the expectations of your online faculty?" "How much emphasis do you put on professional experience versus academic experience?" "How many courses do you currently offer online?" (Only ask this if it isn't a fully online school!) "What are your top priorities for new facilitators?" "What is your university's teaching philosophy?" "What is your enrollment/drop rate compared with other schools?" "How am I evaluated as a faculty member?" "Do you allow your faculty to teach for other schools?" The list goes on, but just as in a traditional job or business interview, you need to engage the faculty or school representatives here. Asking questions gets them to ask more about you and learn more about you, which is a good thing.

Warning: Traditional universities may not take kindly to your being a professional adjunct, as they fully expect that beyond your professional job, their students are your only students and you are loyal to the university. This means you must be careful about how you market yourself to them. Before you think that all of this bureaucracy makes it not worth your time, think again. Your resume will look far more impressive when you are a faculty member of a major university such as Stanford, MIT, Georgia Tech, or the University of Texas. Just be prepared to address the issue of whether you intend to teach for other schools. Job experience is good, but so is loyalty, so depending on the school—toe the line.

Whew! Sounds like a lot of work, and it is, but this is the exception rather than the rule. Most of your interviews will be with nontraditional universities (such as the University of Phoenix, which has both ground-based and online courses, or Capella University, which is 100 percent online), or community colleges that offer online courses.

Nontraditional Universities and Community Colleges

The two don't seem to fit together, but they do in more ways than you might think. Yes, community colleges have traditional daytime students and full-time faculty and real campuses and standard semesters, while nontraditional universities often have no full-time faculty, all adult students, and mostly night/weekend classes, and work out of an office building. What these institutions do have in common, though, is that they often have open enrollment with no limit on the number of students they admit, and they both reach out to adult learners. As such, they are always hiring online faculty. As we discuss in this book, you need to get your applications to the right people up front, and if they are interested in you, they may fast-track you.

Often the process for interviewing is quick because the school doesn't have the manpower to go through a formal process with every applicant. You will probably receive a phone call from a single person, probably the department chair or dean, and he or she will ask a few key questions about your skills, your background, your availability, and your flexibility, and will then give you a chance to ask questions. You may be asked specifically about your online teaching experience and whether you've used the school's platform, which is its online classroom system (discussed in Chapter 9 in greater detail). You can use this as an opportunity to find out more about the university, the pay, the commitment required of online professors, and how scheduling works. If you hit it off, you can expect to advance to the next round—training—rather quickly.

The big-name traditional universities seldom have this formal training because they don't hire faculty with great regularity, but these open enrollment programs tend to take hundreds of applications each week and select a small percentage for consideration. Don't take it too lightly; the training itself is part of the interview process. Your e-mail and written correspondence as well as your verbal skills on the phone are being evaluated, but it is when you participate in the standard online training that you are truly being interviewed, albeit very subtly. This is the area where many potential faculty members are weeded out; they essentially waste many weeks of their time in training only to never be offered a position.

The training courses usually include one on the Web platform and another on general university policies, and sometimes another on the proper way to teach online (i.e., doing things the university way). Sometimes these training modules are rolled up into one or two courses, if you are lucky. One of the established faculty members (sometimes an adjunct) facilitates the course, and you *must* participate like a real student in a real course. This means full participation—if the school requires five days per week of participation, then you must be there five days per week. You are actually graded on your written assignments, your timeliness, your online courtesy, your ability to work in groups, and whether you fit into the culture of the university. A tracking tool is used to see how often you actually log in to the course.

The online training programs use discussion forums just like the courses that you will facilitate if you get the job. In the discussion forums, expect to see questions like "How would you deal with a student who plagiarizes?" or "Should there be a forced grade distribution?" They may also give you real-life situations to respond to—situations like "Joe asks for three extra days for his assignment due to health reasons. Based on university policy, what would your answer to Joe be? Construct a formal letter to Joe and post it in the discussion thread." These questions are not there just to give you practice on the platform; they are there to interview you and to see how you respond to other comments with which you may or may not agree.

At the close of the course, the course facilitator will make a recommendation as to whether you should or should not teach for the university. Don't let your guard down for one minute. This doesn't mean you should worry about the training—it is not difficult and often the routine is similar throughout the nontraditional universities; but it is unpaid time that you must sacrifice with serious effort. If you save your work and discussion responses, you may find them helpful in the next course at the next university. More about training will be addressed in the next chapter.

Faith-Based Universities

If you are a person of faith and would welcome the notion of being able to discuss and mention topics that are off-limits at some schools, then you should consider applying to one of several faith-based universities that have opened their world to online learners. Since we are both Christians, we are most familiar with Christian colleges and they are discussed in this faith-based section of the chapter. However, you should look for schools that match your particular faith if you would like to. While faith-based schools often don't pay as well as secular ones, they can be more rewarding in other ways and worth the effort.

Indiana Wesleyan University and Liberty University are among the most traditional Christian universities in the country. You can expect such faith-based universities to hold faculty, including adjuncts, to a strict philosophical and religious standard. At Liberty University, for example, if your initial e-mail sparks interest, you can expect to receive a seven-page application that is unlike any you have ever seen. You must consent to a background check, provide a detailed statement of faith, provide a letter of reference from a pastor, and respond to several tough questions. Liberty posts its requirements online (at www.liberty.edu/ administration/humanresources/index.cfm?PID=4544), asking for the following:

1. Write a biographical sketch. Include how you came to faith in Christ for salvation and your subsequent spiritual growth, your church involvement, how you came to your particular academic discipline, and your personal goals both as an educator and a professional in your field.

2. Why do you wish to teach at Liberty University?

3. At Liberty we are committed to the objective nature of truth and values as reflective of the nature and character of God. Accordingly we strive to integrate biblical content and a Christian worldview into every classroom and discipline. If you are in agreement, please comment on how these commitments make a difference in the teaching of your discipline. As you do so, please describe your understanding of the following:

   - The Objectivity of Truth and Values
   - The Truthfulness (inerrancy) of the Bible
   - The Existence of God
   - The Creation of the Universe
   - The Image of God in Humankind
   - The Reality of Salvation through Christ
   - Eternal Rewards and Punishment (heaven and hell)

4. Are there any items in the three central documents [Doctrinal Statement, Philosophy of Education, Statement of Professional Ethics] with which you may disagree, do not understand, or on which you desire clarification prior to any possible interview(s)?

Indiana Wesleyan University also posts its application online (at https://secure.indwes.edu/APS/Faculty Application/application/html), and asks for the following:

How would you explain the purpose of Christian Higher Education?

Indiana Wesleyan University's Facilitators are encouraged to integrate scriptural truth with the concepts of the discipline they represent. How might you integrate scriptural truth into your discipline? How would students know you had done so?

How has salvation and acceptance of Christ as your Savior affected your life?

How might your personal Faith in Jesus Christ be evident and applied to the classroom activities?

List any personal ministry, church involvement, or spiritual growth that has been important to you during the past year.

Obviously, these questions require more time and more thought-out answers than "How would you handle Joe's situation with his homework being late?" In addition, many Christian schools may ask you to sign that you are committed to making a difference, based on their philosophy, through teaching. You must state unequivocally that you agree to their truth and values (such as the Bible being the direct word of God), and that you are committed to living your life in a Christlike way. Christian colleges will often ask you to make this statement of testament and of faith. They may include the existence of God, God as the creator of the universe, the reality of salvation through Christ, and punishment (Heaven and Hell).

Needless to say, if you do not believe in these philosophies, you will not fare well here, nor should you even apply. However, whatever your faith, chances are there is a faith-based school that is looking for faculty. Do some online searches and then the answers to the questions they ask will come naturally to you.

After your application packet, your transcripts, and your letters of reference arrive at the school, you can expect one or more phone interviews. The phone interviews can be rather intense; however, usually the people you talk with are quite pleasant. Expect to be asked more about your faith, to make a personal testament on the phone, and to discuss your ability and method of integrating faith with traditional learning.

What to Expect: What Do Deans Want?

What do deans really want in an adjunct? Think of it like computer dating—you want the perfect mate, but you settle for someone pretty good. After all, it is just a date. If it were marriage, you would have stricter standards. The same holds true for adjunct faculty. Adjuncts are the equivalent of a computer date, while tenured faculty members are married to the school. Since you wouldn't date someone without some form of an interview process, whether it is in person, on the phone, or through some online form, you shouldn't expect to get a teaching position without one.

As with anyone you would willingly date, there are qualities you look for in such a person—"must have," "preferred," "nice to have," and "can live without." Deans likewise each have such a unique list for their ideal choice, although some qualities are common to most deans' lists. Let's first look at the "must haves." You can expect all schools to want you to be qualified to teach for them; this means having the required number of graduate semester hours from an accredited college, and those hours need to be in the subject you will potentially be teaching. You can also expect all schools to want you to have your own computer with internet access, and that you have a decent command of the English language. Each of these qualifications should come out in your cover letter, transcript, and phone interview. If you fail to meet any of these standards, don't expect to be an adjunct professor anytime soon.

Probably the most common "preferred" quality that deans seek is prior teaching experience. You will even see the word "preferred" in many job ads for online professors. Yes, there are those few online programs that are strict about not hiring you to teach for them without prior teaching experience; they don't want you to be cutting your teeth on their students. If they really like you, they may even tell you to go teach a couple of courses

124

at a community college and then call them back in a few months, but most often they won't even consider you. Thankfully for many of you, experience is not a "must have" in most schools . . . yet!

Depending on the school, your personality may be an issue. In a smaller or more prestigious university, you can expect the dean to look for the best fit with the faculty. This is not stated in any job description or advertisement, but administrators would like to see certain types of faculty in their school, in part to keep the peace with the tenured faculty, but mostly to protect the reputation of the school. The larger online programs and community colleges can ill afford to be too picky, as they have many slots to fill. The fact that you are qualified is critical; the fact that you are a pleasant conversationalist is unimportant, especially since they are not likely to talk with you after the interview, nor are your students, who will communicate with you primarily via an online forum.

Another "preferred" quality is that you be responsive. How quickly you respond to the dean's e-mails and phone calls will set part of the tone in the hiring process. You might think this should be a required trait, but if you teach a subject that is hard to fill, a lot can be overlooked. So unless you like to teach the subjects that most dread, it helps to be pleasant and responsive. It is wise to find your niche and do some research, finding out how much in demand your particular qualifications are.

Topping the "nice to have" list is that you are a published author. There are those few schools that are currently using publications as a tiebreaker for hiring adjuncts, but they are rare, for now. Getting published looks great on your application; it makes the school look better, and the tenured faculty tend to accept you more easily (although you are not likely to meet them anyway if you just teach online). This does not show up on job ads, but you want to include your publications and conference presentations in your application if you have any. If you have your own web site, be sure to have a presentations section; it is even better if you can videotape any on-ground presentations you have.

Another "nice to have" is patience. You won't get a class every semester, quarter, or whatever term system the university is on. If you are happy to sit on the bench and wait to be put in the game, never complaining, you will eventually be in the starting lineup on a regular basis. However, you must keep yourself visible without nagging. If you nag the dean about when your next class is being offered, don't expect to earn brownie points. Obviously it is important that you stay visible, but you cannot annoy the leadership team every time your class gets canceled for low enrollment, you are asked to teach a directed study due to a small number of students for low pay, or you don't get a class for three months. This goes hand in hand with another "nice to have"—flexibility.

If you are willing to teach anything, anywhere, anytime, you will be on every dean's dance ticket. Their job can be quite difficult, considering that they have to find instructors, schedule classes, keep tenured faculty smiling, deal with student complaints, and evaluate faculty. In addition, many online schools strive for accreditation, which can be a nightmare to obtain. The less of a burden you are and the more you come across as the answer to a dean's problems, the more likely you will become a go-to faculty member.

If you can address several items on the perfect adjunct list of every dean, you will not have a problem finding work as an adjunct. However, if you insist on enhancing that list with other qualities about yourself, beware! Some "can live without" qualities may sound great but can actually hurt you or get you ignored. Keep your politics, religion, and even favorite sports teams out of your correspondence unless it is apparent that mention of them can help; for example, if the dean happened to attend your alma mater, you can certainly milk that for what it is worth. In a faith-based school, it is a sure bet that you can safely discuss religious issues, and can even delve into politics as they pertain to family issues or as they relate to the religion you subscribe to (so long as it's the same as the school's). This type of dialogue can score you points, but if you are not careful it can instead cost you dearly. Remember that you are being hired to teach a course that the school needs to be taught; your favorite baseball team and your opinion on an issue like border patrol are not germane and should be kept in reserve until after you get the job and feel a sense of comfort with your boss and colleagues. Even then, some wouldn't recommend it.

When it comes to what the dean wants, actions speak louder than words. You can write what you are all about, and, except for your credentials generated from your transcripts, everything else will come out in your personal correspondence. How quickly you reply, the tone of your messages, the professionalism of your documents, the openness and availability you make clear, and so forth will tell the dean whether you are a candidate worthy of a first date. The discussion forums of the mandatory training will often set you up to show more of your personality, and that is where you must curb yourself so as not to give away too much about yourself. Remember that in a class of 20 someone is bound to not agree with you, so you should restrict your opinions to class materials only. Talk about relevant issues like retention, how important communication with learners is, and how critical it is for adult learners to feel as though their life experience matters in class. After all, an opinionated person will often be seen as someone that others cannot work with and someone who will try to bring up controversial topics in class or use the classroom as their soapbox. Once you earn the deans' trust and respect, they will be coming to you for your opinions, but show that you are willing to do things their way first.

On the Inside Track: From the Mouth of a Dean

Dr. Maria Puzziferro, Director of Continuing Education at Colorado State University, Denver Campus, oversees the online programs at the college, including recruiting, screening, hiring, scheduling, and evaluating adjunct faculty. She routinely receives hundreds of applications for online faculty positions that she must sift through, and she has hundreds of online courses to manage. In an interview, she shared some of her personal insights about her role as an online dean.

What qualities does she look for in new hires?

Dr. Puzziferro gauges them for several attributes. Her goal is to hire faculty who are in tune with the types of students they have. She tries to determine if the applicant has the skill set to breathe life into online students through a lengthy semester or motivate them in a course that can often be tiring. She sees many applicants who think they can teach online because it appears to be just like exchanging e-mails, but she knows that it takes an engaging and dedicated person to truly be a successful adjunct faculty member at her college.

What is the goal of the interview questions she asks?

Dr. Puzziferro asks questions such as "What challenges do you think online students face?," "What makes for a good discussion question versus a bad one and why?," and "What is your philosophy regarding cheating in online courses?" She avoids canned questions that are common at many schools so she can judge candidates' ability to think and she can truly assess them, and not their prepared responses, when she catches them off guard.

How does she evaluate performance beyond instructor evaluations?

As with any online program, there are personnel assigned to monitor courses at different times throughout the semester. Her team has a checklist by which she evaluates each instructor in each course. First-time faculty members are assigned a mentor who shadows them and watches their every move, and gives feedback throughout the term. Beyond that, instructors are checked regularly to ensure they follow college policies and they are doing their jobs effectively. This is her primary means of evaluating online faculty.

How seriously are instructor evaluations taken?

They are not taken too seriously. Unfortunately, the response rate on evaluations is quite low, with only the most upset students completing a form. Often they fill out an evaluation because of dissatisfaction with a grade, even if totally deserved, while excellent students do not bother to offer praise. As such, it is not fair to pay attention to the ratings on these forms; however, Dr. Puzziferro does pay attention to specific comments if they are serious in nature or repeated by others. To balance out the picture, she looks at the number of grade appeals filed by students in a class as well as the enrollment in the class from day one to the end, paying specific attention to the rate of withdrawal, which is often a bad sign. She also has personnel whose job it is to peek at the online courses regularly and do quality checks; these evaluations are taken very seriously.

What responsiveness level does she expect from adjuncts, and how does she gauge it?

While a 24 to 48-hour response time is expected, it is nearly impossible to measure it. She must rely on student complaints to determine if a faculty member is not being responsive enough, and no news is good news.

Dr. Puzziferro also discussed how hard people work to get hired as adjunct faculty only to lose the job so easily. After dealing with an application process, a series of interviews, eight-week training, and being shadowed in a course, many new adjuncts drop the ball and fail to do the job they promised to do. If only they worked half as hard to keep the job they worked so hard to get, there would probably not be a need for so much recruiting and hiring.

Addressing Your Strengths

There are some basic rules to remember when applying to teach online for a university. (1) As with any job, you get only one chance to make a first impression. (2) Teaching what you want is not as important as teaching what the school needs. (3) Knowing your weaknesses is actually considered a positive. (4) It doesn't matter what you think you can teach—you must have the credentials to back it up. (5) It is better to be the subject matter expert in one important subject than to be just a good jack-of-all-trades. (6) Academic skills may get you in the door, but interpersonal skills will keep you there.

Rule 1: *You Get Only One Chance to Make a First Impression as a Professor*

The first course you teach at a university may be your last or your only. It is important that you start out on the right foot. You need to know what you are capable of teaching and let the school know it. You want to shine bright, and what better way to do so than by teaching something that you excel at? That said, if your niche is very specialized, like world history as it relates to nineteenth-century architecture, you might create a problem for yourself. Keep your topics broad while focusing on what you're good at. There is a fine line to walk here. When they see the added value you bring to the program, your value will rise. You are far more likely to get excellent student evaluations when you know your subject matter—and yes, it does come through online. Student evaluations may not be too important for long-time adjuncts who have proven themselves during years at a university, but rookies may be scrutinized thoroughly, depending on the institution.

Rule 2: *Teaching What You Want Is Not as Important as Teaching What Is Needed*

If you are picky, are inflexible about teaching only a specific course or two, you may be in for a long wait. Different schools have different needs. You need to bend somewhat, within reason. Suppose your strength may be in compensation, but the need is for someone to teach human resource management, which is closely related. If you are willing to jump in and bail the school out, you will then be in the rotation and can request to teach compensation at a future time. The school is not seeking to find a class to suit you; it is seeking faculty to fit the courses being offered. This is very similar to job hunting in the business world. You would rarely just send a blanket e-mail to a CEO saying, "This is what I can do; find a job for me." Rather, you'd apply to a specific position that is open. When you introduce yourself, you also introduce your skill set. The leadership within the organization immediately begins thinking of the courses that need to be taught by adjuncts, and then attempts to potentially match you. Often they'll send a list of courses that need to be taught and ask what your comfort level is teaching them.

Rule 3: Knowing Your Weaknesses Is Actually a Strength

Don't be ashamed of being weak in a subject area. It is far better to know your weaknesses and avoid them than pretend that they are not weaknesses and give an unrecoverable first impression. If the dean begs you to teach out of your comfort zone, he or she should be made aware of the risk you're taking. This happens more than you might think when schools can't fill high-demand courses in tough subjects. You can expect incredible support as you struggle with teaching the course, and it will be to your benefit to continue. Sometimes instructors even have to do their own research to address student questions; while this isn't ideal, it's acceptable in some circumstances. Often the dean will owe you a favor, and then you can expect to get your choice of courses and a reputation for being a team player. This only comes from being open about your weaknesses, or at least not biting off more than you can chew because of exaggerating your expertise.

Rule 4: It Doesn't Matter What You Think You Can Teach—You Must Have the Credentials to Back It Up

Some online professors might think they can teach a course in information technology just because they can use a computer and surf the Web, but without 18 graduate hours in IT, you are not academically qualified. You may know all of the bones in the human body, but you need 18 graduate hours in biology or a related science to teach anatomy and physiology. One of the reasons there is a degree of job security in being an adjunct professor with a doctorate (as is the case for both of us) is that anyone who thinks they can teach our courses cannot just take our jobs away—they must put in the years and earn a doctorate with 18 graduate hours in our subject areas, and then prove themselves from the ground up. What this means to you, though, is to take all of the courses you can in the areas you want to teach so that you are academically qualified.

Rule 5: It Is Better to Be the King or Queen in One Important Subject Than to Be Just a Good Jack-of-All-Trades

Think about the star quarterbacks, pitchers, goalies, and point guards you have known about. Now think about the utility players who can do it all. Whatever the sport, you can probably name the millionaire stars who play a single position, but the utility players are often on the bench, never get invited to all-star games since they are not known for any one position, and make run-of-the-mill salaries. It is not that deans wouldn't like to have a utility player who can teach everything, but when it comes to staffing a course they want the best at each course; and if you are not among the best, you may not be high enough on any list. Yes, the deans will tell you that they appreciate having you around, but the consistent teaching opportunities go to the superstars in each course; so try to become one. When they start calling you the subject matter expert (SME), you will know that you have found your niche there. However, that doesn't mean that if your MBA specialization was in IT you aren't qualified to teach general management courses. You still have an MBA, so try to match your skill set to courses.

Rule 6: Academic Skills May Get You in the Door, but Interpersonal Skills Will Keep You There

Once you are teaching for a university, do what you can to make yourself shine. Communicate with key personnel at the university, including some clerical ones. Let them remember that you are alive, but not to the point of nagging. Don't forward jokes or any potentially controversial e-mails unless you have established a bond that dictates this to be acceptable behavior. If you are good at researching articles, send some links to useful ones for the dean to share with other faculty. If you have some best practices, share them. If you are published, humbly let your boss know. Participate in the school's faculty discussion forum if that is your thing. Volunteer for committees that you can comfortably handle. Agree to write an occasional article for the school newsletter. Network with your colleagues and focus on learning the ways of the current environment.

How you work with others will often dictate your status at the school. If you are someone who doesn't like to mingle or who gets opinionated and offensive unintentionally, it is better just to keep a low profile than to give anyone reason to dislike you. Of course you should work to improve such interpersonal problems, but for now the key is to maintain job security.

These are the key rules to keep in mind. Teaching online is not too difficult; getting hired to teach online is a bit more challenging; making a living at it requires a myriad of skills that take time to develop and master. Reading this book is but the first step.

What to Do with Limited Experience

Many of you are reading this book because you want to teach, but you don't have much experience. Surprisingly, lots of different activities can count for teaching experience by universities' standards. The key is that you can't be too picky with regard to which schools you teach at in the beginning. If you have limited experience, play up any of these activities (and anything else you can think of):

- *Experience on the job training peers.* Write this in your resume with regard to the actual responsibility you had for their learning. If you've ever conducted a computer-based training course or taught a group of people how to do something on a computer or in any particular area, note this as experience training people.

- *Experience as a presenter of new ideas or rollouts of new company plans.* You can easily discuss the way you trained everyone on the new process, solicited feedback, shared ideas, and then communicated to others.
- *Experience making presentations to groups.* This may include professional organizations, your own business, previous courses you were involved in, or seminars.
- *Experience guest lecturing at universities.* If you don't have any, e-mail the faculty at universities who teach in your area of expertise and volunteer yourself. Most will jump at the opportunity and within weeks you will have additional experience for your resume specifically in academia. Even offer to host someone's class for a field trip if your place of business would suit the course.
- *Experience hosting brown bag lunches or conducting speaking engagements at the office, if you are a professional.*

The key here is that if you don't have experience teaching at a school you will have to be creative, but under no circumstances should you blow your experience out of proportion or be dishonest. All of us started somewhere.

Proving Responsiveness

It may feel like a fishing expedition to apply to teach online at any one school, but once in a while you get a bite—a real, human-generated, they-are-interested-in-you e-mail. Sometimes you will get an auto-generated response which puts you in a holding pattern, and sometimes you'll get one that instructs you to take further action. It is critical that you know what cards you have been dealt so you know how to play the hand. There are four basic kinds of e-mails you can expect to see from your efforts.

134

Response 1: Auto-Generated Rejection

If you submitted an application on the university's web site, you can always expect some type of auto-generated response. A common one reads like this: "Thank you for your interest in teaching for Whatsamatta U. Unfortunately, I don't have any openings at this point but you will definitely be considered for courses in the spring semester." Or something like this: "Dear Sir/Madam, Thank you for your application for the position of Adjunct Professor at Whatsamatta U. We did receive a large number of applications for this position, resulting in a very stringent selection procedure. Regretfully, you have not been selected to participate in the training at this time." It may also say that your resume is in a database and that you'll be contacted when there is a match, although the actual likelihood of this happening has been slim in our experience. If you get either of these responses, don't keep your hopes up. Yes, there is a chance that you can still get hired by getting in touch with the right person, but your file has already been put in the reject pile or the official HR database, and chances are no one will be calling you. If you have a friend on the inside who can put you in touch with the right person, take a shot; otherwise, you are probably better off moving on.

It is not uncommon for an experienced, well-educated, highly qualified candidate to be rejected, while an inexperienced recent graduate gets hired. Sometimes these schools pay poorly and they know they are wasting their time to recruit highly qualified professors who are used to being paid well. Their goal is to give experience to new faculty in return for low salaries. (This isn't bad for you if you have no experience; it is a way to add to your resume.) Unless you are willing to work for low pay in exchange for experience, you wouldn't want to teach at these schools anyway, so don't be upset to get a rejection letter. Another common occurrence is to be rejected because you are teaching for a major competitor (although this is not directly disclosed to you). It is up to you what goes on your resume, but with the networking that goes on in the online teaching world, if you teach more than an occasional course for a school, your name may get around, so be careful not to try to hide too much. After all, you must show that you are capable of teaching online, and that is best shown by teaching for other online schools.

Response 2: Auto-Generated Acknowledgment

Another common auto-generated response you might get after applying at the university's web site might read like this: "Thank you for your interest in our opening! Our recruiters have received your resume and will be reviewing it shortly. If your skills and qualifications match our opening we will be sure to contact you. We appreciate your interest in our organization." If you see such a message, do not feel like you are as good as hired, even if you are an accomplished writer, are an experienced faculty member, and have a PhD. Either a computer or a clerical person will determine if you are qualified for further review, and that often is tied to whether you put specific buzzwords in your application. These are not rocket scientists with a thesaurus, but instead typically low-paid, often uneducated clerks who are told to pass along potential candidates to teach a specific subject, like computer science; if your application mentions PC, IT, and information systems, but never uses the word *computer*, you might just get overlooked. With the hundreds or thousands of applications they must review, they are just looking for quick matches, not necessarily the best fits. The lesson here is to try to use a lot of different terms to maximize your chances of success, but not to look as though you're a jack-of-all-trades and a master of none. As far as the e-mail goes, do not respond to it since your response wouldn't go to anyone specific. At this stage, you should follow the advice provided in this book and seek out the deans, course directors, or faculty chairs and send personal e-mails indicating that you have already applied online (mentioning this is important since they will often direct you to do this anyhow, and it shows that you are proactive). Also tell them of your specific teaching interests, and attach your resume and scanned transcripts so they don't have to go through the database to get them.

Response 3: E-Mail from Recruiter

If you are lucky enough to have your e-mail score a hit in the online application process, you can expect an e-mail from a recruiter. It may go something like:

> Hi Jim!
>
> Thank you for your interest in teaching opportunities with Whatsamatta U. We are interested in developing long-term relationships with superior instructors who possess high professional standards, excellent communication skills, enthusiasm, and a commitment to teaching and learning. We look for individuals who hold a minimum of a master's degree (in some areas a PhD is preferred), several years of teaching experience in higher education, as well as significant professional experience in the field in which they teach. We have a strong commitment to delivering high-quality courses. To that end, courses are developed centrally and delivered by our instructors. In addition to the minimum qualifications listed above, new online instructors are expected to:
>
> - Provide official transcripts for each degree earned.
> - Participate in a three-day asynchronous online assessment of their facilitation skills, which can take up to six months to schedule.
> - Work proactively and cooperatively with new faculty trainers during the period of course preparation and course delivery.
> - Ensure compliance for online instruction.
> - Participate in the New Online Faculty Training Program.
>
> Upon successful completion of training, new online instructors are expected to:
>
> - Spend four to five days per week online (including one day on the weekend) for a minimum of 30 minutes each day managing their

137

course delivery. This is in addition to the grading of homework and other course deliverables.

- Work with new faculty trainers who monitor and evaluate their week-to-week activity and effectiveness in managing the delivery of their course.
- Have simultaneous access to both Internet and phone.

If, after reviewing the expectations above and making a realistic assessment of the time you have available, you are still interested in applying for an online teaching assignment, follow these steps:

1. Visit www.whattsamatta.edu and view our catalog and course descriptions.
2. Choose up to a maximum of three courses that you are interested in and feel qualified to teach.
3. Complete the attached Faculty Qualification Form for each course you have chosen.
4. Submit the form(s) and a copy of your resume and any other information you think appropriate for us to review to recruiter@mye-mail address.com.

Again, thank you for your interest and we look forward to hearing from you!

If you should get such a reply, then you are officially being eyed. At this point you should not waste a moment. Go to the catalog and find courses you can teach. It is best if you pick courses that are sure things for you (i.e., courses that you have a lot of graduate credits in, courses that relate heavily to your work experience, and courses that match your prior teaching experience—particularly if the school has disclosed the types of instructors it is looking for). Don't worry about teaching other subjects; once you are hired, you can suggest your other strengths, but you must get in the door first, and so you must impress the recruiter as much as possible and as quickly as possible. If you are unable to do the task immediately for some reason, at least reply and thank the recruiter, ensuring him or her that you will complete the required tasks in the next week. Note: It is going to take a couple of weeks to get your transcripts, anyway, but you should at least impress the recruiter with your responsiveness; it will go a long way.

Response #4: Expression of Interest from Key Personnel

If you made direct contact with key personnel and sparked some interest, they will likely tell human resources that they want your file, and the wheels will start turning. This is the way it works best, and it is by far the most direct and expedient manner by which you can be hired. The e-mail you will get is not standard by any means, but essentially expresses interest. For example, one e-mail that Dr. Mirabella received began:

> Dear Dr. Mirabella,
>
> I received your very impressive resume, and I was interested in seeing if we might be a fit for a position we're seeking to fill this year. I would appreciate it if you would send me [miscellaneous documents listed here]. As soon as I hear back from you, I look forward to seeing about either a full-time or adjunct distance learning position. Finally, I was interested to see your background with the Air Force Academy. As a 26-year veteran of the U.S. Army, I spent eight of my last nine years in uniform at West Point, and I recall fondly some visits I made to Colorado Springs. Have a wonderful week, and thanks for getting back with me.

You can see the personal connection made here. Writing to these people should be more than a form letter, as it can carry a lot of weight if done correctly. This letter basically means that the teaching position is yours to lose, but don't become so overconfident that you cause yourself harm. You have made a strong first impression, but the next step is critical because they still have not seen your responsiveness. Get back to them immediately. Dr. Mirabella replied within two hours and received a further reply, which began "Thanks for your prompt reply!" This shows a genuine interest that cannot be assessed from your transcripts or resume. Consider that you have just received your first exam and earned an A+, but there are more exams to come, so don't let up. Just take solace in knowing that, even if the hiring process is objective, it doesn't hurt to give yourself a subjective edge in the eyes of the decision maker. Be sure to thoughtfully respond to each message, and do so promptly.

What you should take from this is the need to act quickly. If you have a busy week or you're about to take a cruise, then postpone submitting applications or sending e-mails until you can properly deal with responses to them. Unless you are fighting an application deadline for a posted position (this almost never happens online), it is far better to wait to apply when you have some free time and then respond quickly to e-mail requests from the school. You may even want to spread out the applications a few days apart so as not to get hit with numerous requests at once. It is up to you, but be prepared to respond immediately or you may never be able to recover this lost opportunity to add to your online teaching repertoire.

Odd Requests and How to Handle Them

When you do receive a reply from a school, often the school will want more from you than you have already provided. You can expect to see requests for transcripts, letters of reference, faculty qualification forms, and the university's official online application (if you haven't already completed it). You may also receive some less common requests, such as a statement of your teaching philosophy or that you complete an attached interview form with some tough questions. The most annoying by far are the faculty new hire packets you'll receive in the mail with all of the information asked for all over again. Prepare to spend at least an hour filling them out, and even possibly having them notarized.

Transcripts are a guaranteed part of every application process. Save yourself some money and do not send official transcripts until the school requests them from you. You should have a scanned version of your transcripts available on your computer so you can e-mail them and give the school an early look at your qualifications. To hasten the process of getting transcripts, you should visit the web site for every college you graduated from and download their transcript request forms (often a PDF file). This way you can just open the files on your computer, fill them in, print them, and send them to the colleges with the correct dollar amounts. Make sure you find out exactly where to have the transcripts sent, and they must be sent directly to your target school to be counted as official. If your alma mater doesn't offer such a thing, then have your form letter typed up based on the registrar's requirements, fill in the blanks for the school it needs to be sent to, and enclose your check. Usually the target school will receive them in 10 to 14 days, which is expected.

When it comes to your references, you can expect a request either for a list of your references or for actual letters from your references. You should already have prepared a list, and be sure to let these people know when you use them as references so they are not surprised and they commit to supporting you. If you're in a particular profession, let your references know you're trying to get a teaching job so they don't talk about how great you are in the boardroom, but instead how well you trained the teams and what a great teacher you'd make. If you are asked for a letter of reference, that can be quite a demand for anyone; your best bet is to write a letter for each person to sign, allowing them to edit to suit their tastes, or ask the same individuals so they may use the same letter but address it to a new school. Make sure the wording on each letter is quite different and speaks from the perspective of that person's knowledge of you. If they e-mail you their letter, you can save it for future use and just change the date and name of the school each time you use it; if the school expects the letter to be mailed (which is rare these days), then you must ask your friends to print, sign, and mail the letters. Once you get a core set of references with letters written, this part of the process becomes smooth, albeit time-consuming.

If you are asked to complete a faculty qualification form, you are merely going to peruse the school's catalog and find courses you are qualified to teach. Then you must extract related work experience from your resume, add graduate course work from your transcripts, and list any related courses you have taught or developed. It doesn't hurt to list any articles you've had published or any professional organizations of which you are a member (e.g., Academy of Management, Decision Sciences Institute, American Society for Quality, American Statistical Association, etc.). Typically you must complete a separate form for each course, but once you fill out the first one, you can merely save it and edit it for the next course. Choose the courses that will most likely get you hired quickly; this means picking core courses that are offered every term versus an elective that is rarely offered. It also means picking courses for which you have the most graduate credits and teaching experience, which truly count more than work experience when the final decisions are made.

One of the more annoying requests is to fill out the school's online application. You are so tempted to just put "see resume" in the application, but that won't work. This is similar in nature to the faculty new hire packet you'll receive; you may even receive both! They want to enter your data into their database and they don't have the manpower to extract this data from your resume. The good news is that you don't have to worry about getting past the clerical staff for approval; you are just filling this out as a requirement. You still need to invest the hour to do it correctly and to ensure that you included all educational information accurately, as that is what the accrediting body will look at if you ever are at risk of being terminated. Be sure to make a copy of any paper forms you complete or a printout of any online forms you complete. You may find similarities across different schools and you wouldn't want to have to rethink your answers. Plus, in the unlikely event the mail gets lost or your online form doesn't load properly, you can redo it in just a few minutes.

One of the less common requests is for a statement of your teaching philosophy. This is merely a paragraph or two of your personal philosophy with regard to adult learners, online teaching, and education in general. Do you believe everyone is entitled to an education? Do you believe students should have the opportunity to resubmit work until they earn an A?

Whom do you see as the customer? What is your teaching style? These are some of the questions you should ask yourself in this unscripted document. Whatever you write, be sure that it reflects you, your personality, and what you truly believe. You need to be genuine and make sure there is a good fit here.

In the unusual case that you receive an interview form to complete, treat it like an exam that is being graded. Do it quickly and do it well. Be prepared to speak from it during your phone interview, as you will likely be asked questions about your responses. This topic was addressed earlier in this chapter, but it is definitely something to be aware of and prepared for, because although it is uncommon, it is usually an excellent sign that you will get a phone interview if your answers are acceptable to the school.

Whatever request you get, the most important rules of thumb are that you respond quickly and accurately, write professionally, and be true to yourself and your style. It wouldn't be surprising to see more schools devise uncommon requests to separate truly interested applicants from the rest, and we expect to see this as schools juggle more and more online teachers with heavily increasing demands from students.

8

Sealing the Deal, Training, and Your First Class

The mediocre teacher tells. The good teacher explains. The superior teacher demonstrates. The great teacher inspires.
— William Arthur Ward, Author, Editor, Pastor, and Teacher

In the previous chapter, we focused on what to do when you obtain an interview for a school that you want to teach for. In this chapter, we focus on what to do when you are offered a position, subject usually to training. What happens next? What should you expect?

What Next?

First, congratulations on a big step in the process. Not many people make it this far, and to be considered for a position is an honor. Usually at this point you're invited to join the faculty through a formal offer, albeit usually by e-mail and rarely by phone. If you want to work for the school, then you accept. At this point official transcripts will most likely be requested if they haven't been already, and you will be sent a human resources packet with all kinds of goodies to sign and perhaps even have notarized. Fill out the paperwork and return it as soon as possible. Send out any remaining transcript request items, and begin to prepare for training. If this is your first (or even up to your fourth) training course, expect to spend an hour or two per day on it. If you're an old pro, you will probably need less time. Training courses will have requirements for participation, as you'll see in the training section of the chapter, so you need to work the next steps into your schedule.

You'll most likely be introduced by e-mail to several key players at the university, but don't expect to be introduced to anyone higher up than the dean. This is normal. Unfortunately, you will be offered a particular set amount per class or per student and you won't have any negotiation room, particularly if this is one of your first schools.

Salary or Contract Negotiation

The school will tell you what it pays adjuncts, and you have to decide if you want to accept. Some factors that should weigh into your decision include how many courses you expect to teach, what potential the school has for you, its reputation among faculty, and of course how you feel about the university. If the pay is insanely low, as it is at some schools, don't be reluctant to say no and politely explain why. Sometimes there will be a counteroffer, but this is rare and usually happens only if the school really needs you and has no one waiting in the queue with a class pending. This is a good situation for the adjunct, but you also don't want to start off on a bad foot with your new boss. It might be best if you're new to online teaching to take what you are given and begin building your online reputation, adding some experience to the resume. This is for you to decide based on your goals, where you are in your career, and how badly you want to work for the school. Be aware that a really high offer may not be so high when you consider the extra unpaid work you'll have to do.

After you decide whether to accept or reject the offer, consider this a done deal. Unless the entire university raises pay (often due to low retention rates and faculty surveys complaining about pay), your salary or contract amount will remain constant. Since we are not employees, in all but the rarest of cases we are not given cost-of-living adjustments or random raises. If you need more money next year, you need to teach another class or two.

There may be some areas of your contract that are negotiable; read through them but beware—deans and chairs do not expect that you will complain or even ask about any portion of the contract. Ask what you really need to know and truly need clarification on, and then make a decision either way quickly. A lot of e-mails flying back and forth make you appear ungrateful and will just upset people. Asking intelligent questions (and collecting them all for one, short, bullet-point e-mail) is appropriate, and most administrators at schools will be thankful you asked up front rather than accepting and being upset later.

What to Expect

Now what should you expect? Prepare to wait. You will not usually be able to teach a course without training except in rare circumstances in which a course is beginning right away and there is a desperate need for you. In that case, you may ask to waive training altogether, depending on your experience with the platform the school uses.

The Training Program

After waiting some time, usually a coordinator will e-mail you with a login ID, password, and link to your training course along with the start and end dates. Log in as early as the course will allow so you can get a jump start on training, particularly in noting the workload (this varies greatly by program and university) and introducing yourself to the course facilitator; you also want to be certain that you can access the course before the start date rather than bringing up technical issues when it is too late. Don't expect the facilitator to arrive in the classroom until training actually starts, though, and we caution you against sending e-mails out about an absent trainer if the course hasn't officially started yet. Many are also teachers (sometimes adjuncts like yourself), and some have multiple training classes at one time; they expect you to be self-directed, so be so.

Types of Training

There are several types of training that you will most likely be subject to, as well as multiple types of checks and balances to be sure you are learning what the university intended. It's critical to note that every move you make, every e-mail you write, and every post you make is being graded and judged, with reports usually given to the chair and/or dean. Treat this as you would any important training course for a job; you haven't gotten it yet! You must usually pass training before actually being given a class to teach.

There are a few key points that most universities have in common with regard to goals for training. First, they want you to be intimately familiar with their processes. This sounds simple enough until you start teaching for several schools! It's easy to confuse which date attendance must be turned in with another school's policy, or the grading scales, for instance, or which days you must maintain office hours if required. This is where your organization and technology will come in; you must be prepared to organize yourself and the requirements placed on you. So, intimate familiarity with their process is important. You'll cover ground like "What to do with a tardy student" and "How much flexibility you have granting assignment submissions after their due date." You will go through numerous policies, and some schools will also require that you are familiar with accreditation body rules or some higher authority rules. You will be tested and graded on this. Sometimes you'll need the material later on after you've begun teaching, so save the documents you get from training.

Another goal of training is for you to learn the school's platform. Even if two schools use Blackboard, they may have different features installed. The training for the platform, while having some similarities, will be quite different. Don't simply tell your boss, "I already know Blackboard," and try to get out of training. They are assessing more than your Blackboard skills. They are also assessing your adherence to their way of doing things. If you like having students post assignments in the Assignments section, but a school likes to use the Digital Drop Box, learn to like it; the students will be doing it that way and you shouldn't try to make them adapt to your style.

Finally, most universities use training to try to gauge your responsiveness and your writing capabilities. Reports are frequently sent, and documentation is made in your HR file (yes, you will have one even though you aren't an employee). They will judge your attentiveness, your listening skills (there actually is such a thing online), how you use humor in the classroom, the appropriateness of your responses, and so forth. Treat this as you would any class and take it seriously.

Remember that someone is always watching you; even if they aren't watching at the time you are on, whatever you post online is there for eternity, so they can watch whenever they like. A favorite metaphor is the dreaded driver's license photo—you can hold that smile for only so long, and then when you begin to sneeze, the photo is taken and you are stuck with it for a few years. Well, until you get the notice that you passed your training, keep holding that smile and behave!

Expect two training courses: a practice classroom and a training classroom. The training classroom will have discussions you must participate in (with participation requirements, the most time-consuming part of training); lectures you must read (with rules, processes, and best practices); Q&A; as well as homework, quizzes, and usually a group assignment (by far the most frustrating!). Some schools will let you self-direct your pace and hammer out the entire program in two days if you can. Others will force you through a rigorous and very time-consuming directed process in which you follow a typical class pattern. Either is okay, but obviously one is less demanding because you can get it done all at once.

In addition to the facilitator training forum or class, you will have a practice class in almost every school. The practice classroom is one where you will complete assignments, like "add a drop box item to unit 4" or "add an announcement." This is done with instructor-level privileges only, which you do not have in your training classroom. In the training class, you are a student, seeing what the students see and experiencing what they experience. In your practice classroom, you will have facilitator-level access, which means you can add, delete, and change items in the course. Your assignments will usually require you to perform various tasks, and the syllabus should tell you what portions of the practice class you are graded on.

Try to go overboard in your postings (but keep them substantive in nature); respond to everyone's introductions with a warm, personalized welcome, and respond to every posting that is not directed at another student. While there is a qualitative side to this process in how you do the job, there is an easier-to-assess quantitative side in which your postings are counted and your time in the course room is tracked. Post early, post often, and be professional.

Communicating with Your Trainer

Communicate frequently with your trainer. A weekly summary e-mail is appropriate if grades aren't being posted regularly. Expect to be trained, then retrained, and then retrained again every time the system or a major process changes. It's a part of the job we don't necessarily like and is usually unpaid, but it's part of the deal. Don't complain about it and just do what you need to do.

Sometimes universities (typically the not-so-good ones) will keep you on their list of faculty to make their faculty seem stronger (more PhDs, for instance). You won't hear from them for a while, except when it is time to update your online profile for accreditation purposes. This is okay if you think you may get a class; however, if you haven't for some time, it's entirely appropriate either to have them give you a class or officially resign, forcing them to take your name off of their faculty list. Don't let them benefit from your credentials while you earn nothing. Other universities that you apply at can easily find you at these places via a search engine. You may keep a school off your resume, but you cannot hide yourself from the Web as easily. Associating yourself with an unscrupulous institution can come back to haunt you if you're not careful. Keep on top of your past and present schools as you would your credit report, because essentially your online teaching history is relatively public. You might even do a Google search for yourself to see what others can see (it's actually interesting to see how many hits you have).

Length of Training Process

Training can be anywhere from a self-directed two-hour PowerPoint presentation and an e-mail acknowledgment of understanding to a six-week training class. Some even have additional internships where you must work under an experienced faculty member and respond to his or her concerns about your course. These are the two extremes, with most falling in between, requiring four to six weeks of your time in a directed environment. Sometimes you can work ahead, but often trainers ask that you don't.

If you are asked to participate in an internship as some colleges will have you do, note that although it is frustrating to an experienced faculty member, they are doing it because of either quality concerns, accreditation issues, or both. Just try to work through it, listen to the trainer, and respond to his or her concerns the same day you receive e-mails. Often they will ask you how you would "fix this problem" in a real course and explain to you the gap between policy and what you have done in the internship. It is frustrating to have someone look over your shoulder, but remember that most schools have someone check in to all classes once in a while anyway to make sure that faculty are doing their jobs. It's something you'll just need to get used to.

If there is any chance you may not be able to complete the training per the school's requirements because of a planned trip or because of poor Internet connectivity where you are during that time, let the school know up front. There is no shame to doing this; you have already been selected and are not going to be tossed aside because you need to delay the training. First impressions are everything, so be honest rather than performing poorly and then making excuses afterward. If they really need you desperately, they'll tell you to do the training as scheduled, but will pay less attention to your number of postings and treat it more as a formality. If you were to fail the training course, you would essentially be banned from teaching there, so either give it your all or say up front why you cannot do so.

Proving Yourself to the Trainers and Your Chairperson

After you have proven yourself to the trainer, who usually sends a report to the chairperson, it's appropriate to ask when you might expect a course to teach. Don't expect the trainer to know the answer unless the trainer is also the scheduler, which does happen on occasion. If you don't have a class within a month, set an appointment in your calendar reminding yourself to e-mail your boss asking again about potential scheduling, reminding him or her that you completed training (and include your grade if you got one, and a good one at that!). If you want to feel less intrusive, ask if there is anything else you need to do to move forward to teaching, while reexpressing your interest in the institution.

Prepping for Your First Class

After completing training, you'll need to prepare for your first class. If this is your very first time teaching, it might be a little intimidating. Here are some things almost every university will want you to do. Be sure to pay close attention to the checklists given during training or in the offer to teach (or even in the follow up e-mail after accepting a class). Most will include:

- Post welcome note in the announcements.
- Post bio in the instructor portion of the class.
- Post bio and welcome note in the area students must post theirs.
- Set up the entire grade book such that the point total equals 100 percent.
- Set up discussion boards for at least the first week (though Dr. Babb likes to set up the entire class duration on day one—it keeps things orderly and there is less maintenance).
- Order the textbook and any required software if you don't have them already.

Some not-so-common requests:

- Configure assignment submission settings.
- Update syllabus or post syllabus.
- Send individual e-mails to every student welcoming them (which is a nice touch anyway).
- Check all Web links to make sure the web sites are still there.

It's important that until you have a school's checklist memorized, you go through it every time you receive it. Most will send it at the beginning of each term as a reminder. Some schools even use auditors that log in to make sure you've done everything. Don't let your class be flagged, especially before you have a good reputation (or any reputation). Just follow the rules and eventually you will build rapport. Remember, most of the time classes are replicated so a lot of the data, like lectures and course assignments, remain time and time again. Customization to make your class unique to you is often all that is required to set up a new class.

If this is the first time you have taught a particular class, become very familiar with it so you can answer student questions efficiently. You will need to learn the school's processes and way of doing things and also respond to many requests when the responses are not familiar territory. You'll be learning the system, the culture, the students, the grading policy, and how involved Big Brother is in the process. If permitted, ask if you can peek at another section of the course you will be teaching. You can often contact that instructor and even obtain some excellent ideas for discussion questions and course setup. The other instructor may share some exams and solutions with you, too.

One thing to remember is that you are human and prone to error. There will be mistakes in the course room that you overlooked (such as the wrong due date for an assignment, or poorly worded instructions, or the wrong point value for an exam). If you make a mistake, own up to it and fix it. You can even let the students know that, while you are not new to teaching, this is your first semester with Whatsamatta U. so you are just getting used to the platform, and for them to let you know if they find any errors. Even if you're not new, there are bound to be mistakes made; perhaps you forgot to record an assignment or give a student credit for something. This is no big deal; just be honest and fix it. If the course has some areas for improvement with the design, keep an electronic notebook of the problems so you can fix them the next time you teach the course; the object is to make it better and better until the course practically teaches itself. After about the third or fourth time, you will find it almost effortless, since you will have a bank of standard responses to common questions, few errors, and solutions files already set up.

Finally, and this is very important, come out of the starting gate as very strict but fair. Students may complain about you being tough or demanding, but in the end they fall in line with your requirements and ultimately do well. If you try to be popular, you will find yourself working much harder to please everyone, and you will be dealing with a lot of strange excuses. With a strict grading policy and little forgiveness, as long as clearly stated in the syllabus or faculty expectations message, you will have essentially created a binding contract that the school will support should a student protest your practices as unfair. The rule of thumb is to manage by exception (such as for military deployment or hurricane-related damage), be firm but fair, put everything in writing, apply standards consistently, and be a teacher now and a friend later. Students will respect you first and like you later. If you want to see how you're doing in your students' eyes, review your student feedback or ask the learners for comments.

9

Working as an Online Faculty Member

Better than a thousand days of diligent study is one day with a great teacher.

—Japanese Proverb

Working as an online faculty member—or course facilitator, as many universities call us—is quite different from working within other organizations, even on-ground universities. On-ground universities tend to be somewhat bureaucratic and are slow to change; they also focus on assignment and direction by committees of full-time faculty and administrators, and usually aren't for-profit institutions. Online organizations, by contrast, particularly if they are purely online, like Walden University or Capella University, tend to embrace change and operate more like a business. Institutions that offer both an on-ground program and an online program can often be found operating much like a traditional university.

Working as online adjunct faculty has its pros and cons, as we detailed in the previous chapters. Each university will adopt a system to teach its courses online, and some are easier, while others are more time-consuming or just more annoying.

In this chapter we provide you with several important pieces of information. First, we explain the different types of systems that the universities you work for may choose to adopt. Whatever system the school uses is what you will have to use as the professor. Although each university will offer a training program, it is important to know ahead of time what you may be asked, learn some of the terminology, and understand some of the basic pros and cons of each of the systems.

Second, we show you a pay versus workload matrix that may help you decide where to spend your time and invest your training as you begin to work for various schools. Once you have enough assignments to fill your pockets with the money to pay your mortgage, you can use this matrix to help you determine which schools you want to continue working for and which you want to abandon for better opportunities.

Third, we talk about communication in the classroom and what you can do to make yourself visible to the learners and the advisement teams or department chairs who will probably periodically review your course rooms. This will include a review of feedback, postings, announcements, and several other ways you can make your presence in the classroom known. Remember this is a key to doing your job and for the university to know you're doing it. Unlike in the traditional classroom where you speak once or twice a week and what is said is between you and the students, in an online classroom Big Brother is watching.

Next, we discuss learning what you're good at, documenting it, and doing it really well. This will be the basis for building your reputation and making you an invaluable part of university life at online schools.

We will begin to wrap up this chapter with a review of using e-mail—not the phone—for communicating, unless of course the university you work for specifically requires it. There are several reasons for this, and we go into those in detail. We will conclude this chapter with yet another discussion on life as an adjunct, this time based on all of the new information you have gathered from the first several chapters, and how to balance your work and home life.

Types of Systems—Knowing the Difference

Every university you work for will use one of several systems; after all, like most technologies, there are only so many options. In this section, we run through those systems with which we are most familiar. Since between us we teach for about 15 schools, we can give you a fairly reliable sample of what's out there.

Blackboard

Blackboard has been around for a very long time. It consists today of e-education enterprise software applications and services. Its five software applications are bundled into two suites you may hear of often: the Blackboard Academic Suite and the Blackboard Commerce Suite. The Blackboard Learning System is the most widely adopted course management system in U.S. postsecondary institutions (www.blackboard.com). In 2005, Blackboard announced plans to merge with WebCT, one of the competing companies offering a different product. The new company will remain under the Blackboard brand and will have over 3,700 clients under the new organization. Both the Blackboard and WebCT product line, according to the company web site (www.blackboard.com), will remain supported and intact. What you will mostly see out there is the Academic Suite, which includes the Learning System. This is essentially one of the Blackboard online classrooms. This tool set allows you to run your courses, collaborate, message, have discussions, submit assignments, and so on. Essentially this is the classroom. Blackboard is currently a publicly traded company under the symbol BBBB, and was recognized by the Red Herring Small Cap 100 for its innovative technology (PR NewsWire/Yahoo!, 2005).

The Blackboard Community System is a less popular, though still used, system. This application integrates academic and transaction environments at the university. It is a tool to improve information flow and, as Blackboard puts it, "enhance the sense of community" for those individuals involved (www.blackboard.com).

The Content System is one we've seen used more often, and it's quite intriguing. It will allow a facilitator (that's you) to store information and reuse content without having to reupload every time you facilitate a course. Setting up a course can be very demanding and take a lot of time, and this system helps make that easier. It also helps the university manage content and revisions of courses. Tracking versions of documents is often cumbersome, and this tool helps solve the problem.

From the perspective of the online teacher, Blackboard is as basic as it comes. The newer versions offer some enhancements that allow for some auto-grading procedures to go a little more smoothly than in many of the other systems available out there today. Blackboard has an easy-to-use message board system that allows you to run discussion threads and sort various posts. It doesn't do as good a job as other systems in assisting the facilitator in judging participation from learners based on the number of posts or the content in their posts. The facilitator must actually count posts, read every single post made, and make a determination as to whether participation requirements were met. Universities have various participation requirements, and our job as facilitators (among others) is to make certain these criteria are met. Most students' grades are at least partially dependent on this element, and participation is undoubtedly the most cumbersome grade to assign each week, especially since it is so subjective and therefore worth minimal points.

WebCT

WebCT, which remains as a stand-alone product despite its announced 2006 merger with Blackboard, is another system you will frequently see used out there. WebCT offers Campus Edition and WebCT Vista. Campus Edition is a course management application that offers preparation, delivery, and management of courses online. Vista is the premier version of WebCT's product called the Academic Enterprise System. It's built in such a way that universities can easily create virtual course environments, support diverse operating groups within the same campus, and distribute and reuse content (critical to fast deployment of courses), and it also offers several software development and reporting tools. Rumor has it from many of our colleagues at various institutions that these development tools take days and days to work with and are very difficult and cumbersome, so it could be considered (from the administration's standpoint) as a pro or a con. Sometimes school systems (much like businesses) have no integration among their systems. WebCT has been great with developing systems that allow for the integration of items such as student records, admissions, and advising.

WebCT is implemented in over 70 countries at thousands of institutions (www.webct.com). The company was founded in 1996 and is a privately held organization (at least prior to its merger with Blackboard—we will see what happens next).

From a facilitator's standpoint, WebCT is relatively easy to use and has many features built into it that make automation a breeze. For example, you can review all drop box assignments (these are assignments that are submitted through an electronic submission system) at one time, then grade the assignments, and the grade book will auto-update. WebCT also allows you to control discussions effectively by locking folders after a set date so as to keep the class from adding to outdated discussions; this keeps students focused where you want them to be, while still allowing them to read past postings if they wish. WebCT is not fast, though, even on quick servers, for doing certain tasks like combining all unread messages (yet this is something Blackboard doesn't do within multiple forums at all), and it's rather difficult to learn when compared with the simple Blackboard program. Its grade book is rather difficult to figure out off the bat, and it takes quite a bit of practice to feel comfortable with the system.

eCollege

The third and final specific tool we will talk about, eCollege, provides an integrated approach for distance education programs from an administrative viewpoint. According to its web site at www.ecollege.com, eCollege claims to be the only e-learning outsource provider (keep in mind it is outsourced!) that provides a single point of contact with assurance that the system will be up and running. A public company trading under the symbol ECLG, it was the first publicly traded e-learning company that was focused primarily on the higher education market. It was named on *Forbes'* list of the top 25 fastest-growing technology companies in 2004 and 2005, and was recognized on the 2005 Red Herring Small Cap 100 list based on its innovation and smart business model. It was named Technology Company of the Year by the Colorado Software and Internet Association Apex Awards in 2004, and won numerous other awards presented by respected organizations. In fact, according to *Forbes*, eCollege's stock price has doubled in the past 12 months, and the company appeared on the *Forbes* Fast Tech list again in 2006 (Murdock, 2006, p. 1). No doubt eCollege is a force to be reckoned with.

From our perspective, eCollege is a bit clumsy and a bit difficult to work with. There are separate tabs for the facilitator for authoring a course and actually participating in one. While this makes it easy to switch between modes, as instructors we can't see why we'd even need to do that. When you select a particular area in the classroom you want to modify, you then click on the author tool that will allow you to modify the content there. For instance, if you click on Course Home, you will see announcements. If you then click Author, you can add an announcement. It seems to have many added steps that don't make sense and really could be streamlined for the facilitators. It does have some nice features, such as the ability to set up a drop box that allows you to enter grades into the grade book with ease, much like WebCT. However, also like WebCT, setting up these grade book items is cumbersome at best, and the interface is confusing even for those of us who have been teaching for years. If you're going

162

to work for a university using this system, be prepared for a slow first few weeks while you get the hang of it. If you're asked to develop a course in this platform, you might want to consider asking for a bonus. Blackboard has the easiest grade book to set up by far, but it doesn't have the flexibility of seeing all students' submitted drop box items on one page so that you may grade them and return them to the students without clicking back to the grade book.

Other Systems

The university you work for may choose a proprietary method of serving up courses. Axia and the University of Phoenix use newsgroups, which is a serious pain if you want to use Outlook. There are tools out there that will help you integrate newsgroup support into this application if you need to do so; however, it's not easy. Their platforms require you to have access to a newsgroup reader, and if you choose Outlook Express, they really emphasize its use. However, it also messes with the settings of Outlook Express, and you have to change your default mail outbox, change your settings for spell-checking, and numerous other annoyances. These colleges have yet to implement a system that is user-friendly; however, their system is simple.

Some universities still use Web-based proprietary systems and either are already migrating or have no intention of doing so. Many use systems like Learning Times Elluminate for chatting, or a system built into a Lotus platform for teaching. You might see some companies begin to use Moodle or even instant messaging for chats. Some use a combination of tools, depending on what it is you need to do to meet their course room requirements.

Here are lists of pros and cons to the four main tools mentioned. These are strictly our viewpoints. Anything we disagreed on was left out so that you would get a more accurate depiction of our combined experiences. Also note that the pros and cons are only from the viewpoint of an online teacher, to help you understand what you may be getting yourself into, depending on who you go to work for.

Blackboard

Pros

- If you are new to online teaching, it is extremely easy to learn to use.
- Discussion boards are well laid out.
- Grade book is easy to use and learn.
- Administrative tasks like announcements are easy to set up and the instructor can roll out certain items at a specific time period in advance.
- Quizzes are easy to set up and auto-grade when submitted, saving the instructor a lot of work during class but adding to prep time.
- The content management tool is useful for many people who teach the same courses consistently.
- New versions let you see all of your new items at login so you know where you need to focus your attention.
- The grade book lets you easily manage your grades offline in a spreadsheet and then upload them again at the end of the unit.

Cons

- The ability to view multiple learner drop box assignments, open the files, and submit grades directly into the grade book is cumbersome at best; many of us believe it to be nonexistent.
- Older versions of Blackboard are very limited in their functionality.
- Many universities don't replicate a lot of the data like discussion boards, so course setup can be cumbersome.
- The facilitator cannot collect all messages in all forums that are new at one time and view them together.
- Viewing learner participation to make accurate assessments of their work is nonexistent or difficult to do in Blackboard.
- Discussion folders cannot be locked, hidden, or set to read-only, so it is sometimes difficult to control the flow of discussion.
- E-mail is not self-contained within the course, so you must rely on personal e-mail for private communication.

WebCT

Pros

- The facilitator can collect all messages in all forums that are new at one time and view them together. While it's a slow process, it saves considerable time in a course.
- Discussion threads are extremely easy to set.
- Discussion folders may be hidden, locked, or set to read-only, thereby making it easy to keep the discussion under control.
- Administrative tasks are easy and simplified.
- Integrated messaging and e-mail makes student communication easy.
- There are simple ways to enter feedback, even canned responses, to learners on participation and assignment points.

Cons

- Setting up the grade book can prove particularly difficult and challenging, especially if the university sets participation points and they don't coincide with your grading criteria or syllabus.
- The facilitator (to the knowledge of the authors) has to log out of WebCT and back in again to go to another class or another section of the same class, at least at the universities the authors work at. This can prove particularly annoying and time-consuming.
- Collection of messages, while a nice feature, takes a very long time.
- Learning the system isn't quite as fast and intuitive as others are.

eCollege

Pros

- The course home page lets the facilitator see at a glance what is pending and what forums students have last posted to since the facilitators' last login. If there are questions for you as a facilitator in that forum, for instance, you know immediately upon logging in.
- Drop box items that are graded have grades auto-populated into the grade book.

- Message posts can be easily sorted by author, date, thread, and so on, although replying to them doesn't always return you to the same place you were at prior to opening a message.
- Creating feedback and responses to individuals in each unit is relatively easy, including the use of canned responses.

Cons

- We felt eCollege was the most annoying to use and most difficult to learn of all the systems. It is not intuitive and doesn't offer much in the way of built-in help.
- The facilitator cannot collect all messages in all forums that are new at one time and view them together.
- The facilitator must jump between authoring and viewing a course, which is an extra step and doesn't appear to add any value.
- Adding simple items like notes and announcements takes much longer in this system than in others.
- Unit assignments are difficult to understand, and students have given feedback that of all systems, this is the most difficult to understand and learn.
- Adding an assignment for the drop box is quite an effort, with the grade book being the most cumbersome and lacking intuitiveness.
- It is not easy to add formatting to discussion board posts.
- Posts don't have a separate subject line, but take the first few words off of the message. This makes it very difficult to see what the post is about, a serious drawback particularly if the question is directed to the instructor and requires immediate attention.

Newsgroups

Pros

- Newsgroups are extremely easy to learn to use.
- You don't need to log in to any particular web site, just e-mail or a client.

- If you configure it properly (with a lot of work), you can access the newsgroups from your PDA.
- You can drag and drop canned feedback (and this is recommended in many of the training programs) to save yourself time.
- Newsgroups enable fast posting of announcements, messages, and discussion board topics.
- Threading is easy and it's simple to see what messages are new.

Cons
- Feedback mechanisms take a long time, particularly within some university systems that require Excel spreadsheets to be pasted into the student's newsgroup.
- Managing many newsgroups, up to 20 for each class, can be extremely cumbersome.
- Outlook isn't inherently supported, only Outlook Express.
- Using automated tools can damage settings in Outlook Express, and sometimes it takes weeks to uncover the damage.
- Grading takes a particularly long time.

Time Matrix—Pay versus Workload

Most adjunct faculty members or course facilitators are essentially entrepreneurs who run a business serving students. They work for numerous clients—the universities—and their goal is to maximize their pay for their workload while providing the best service possible. The same business strategies apply to acquiring and keeping a roster of good online schools as just about any other small business, with a few key modifications.

As discussed previously, there are many hidden efforts that can exhaust your time and resources. It's important to find out about as many of these as possible before beginning work with a school, and to also consistently monitor and assess them as you begin working. You might not have the luxury of turning down a teaching job while you're new to the adjunct world and in need of experience, but eventually you will want to balance your life and workload with your pay.

As a refresher, some of the key areas that will eat up much of your time may include committee meetings, faculty meetings, quarterly meetings on updates, and mandatory chats in some online courses, as well as attendance at residencies or colloquia (although you may be paid for these), attending additional (often redundant) faculty development courses, and serving as a mentor for a learner (again you are usually compensated for this, but some schools require more work than others and some schools expect learners to be more self-directed than others). Eventually you will develop your own time matrix, and you will be able to determine where your efforts are best spent. Keep in mind that this is only a picture of time and money, not a picture of satisfaction. Adding the satisfaction and enjoyment you get from teaching can make these pay versus workload considerations irrelevant. Nothing is more enjoyable than being supported by your bosses and having the academic freedom to teach your best. When you are treated like a valued faculty member, as long as you don't feel exploited and the pay is reasonable, you are not likely to evaluate whether it is worth leaving that university for higher pay elsewhere; after all, the biggest reason we teach is because we love it; the income potential just makes it the perfect job for people like us.

Factors That May Affect Your Workload

We have developed, based on our experience, a list of things to look out for that may increase your workload dramatically or cut into your critical teaching time or free time (although some of these can be time well spent). Let's look at some of the major ones to beware of, and then you can begin to utilize the matrix we have provided to help evaluate each school critically and determine whether you want to stay.

- *Micromanagement.* Some universities may micromanage you, checking your time in the classroom, monitoring exactly how many posts you make, and asking you to make numerous administrative changes that don't have an apparent goal. The more they micromanage you, the more time you waste, and this cuts into your earnings potential.

- *Excess training.* It's normal to require training. When rules change or systems change, you need to be retrained, and this will help you in the long run. However, if a school requires constant retraining or training programs more than twice a per year, consider this abnormal. It will increase your workload unnecessarily.

- *Attendance tracking.* Some schools have online attendance tracking by e-mail or some other online tool where you are required to fill out a weekly form for each course you teach; this can be very time-consuming. Other schools ask only that you report students who are absent (which is a small percentage); this is a reasonable request that takes little time and can ultimately save you trouble, since the advisers intervene with regard to those absent students immediately.

- *Mentee tracking.* At the master's and doctoral level, you may be required to report periodically on the status of those you mentor. While this can add to your time spent, chances are that you won't have more than a few to report on and doing so won't be a real drain on you. Also, this may help to nudge some of you to keep in contact with those you mentor more regularly.

- *Self-directed learner mentoring.* Mentoring learners can be extremely satisfying, and even a requirement at some universities. However, do this for schools that require the learner to be self-directed so that you aren't answering process questions, but instead working with the learner to actually learn. If you have to be a hand–holder, you will find yourself investing a lot of time for very small gains (and often you don't get paid unless the learner actually graduates).

- *Conference calls.* Requiring more than a quarterly conference call may be considered excessive by some faculty. It all depends on your patience level and if the calls are productive. As long as you receive valuable information and get to network, consider them time well spent; otherwise they are interfering with your work time.

169

- *Unpaid conferences.* In an effort to create a sense of community, update faculty on policies and procedures, and gain feedback, universities sometimes hold conferences that are unpaid. Your travel may be covered, but your time isn't compensated for in most cases. Usually they are not mandatory, but if they are, expect them to be a drain on your time and your wallet.
- *Faculty lead.* Being a faculty lead can be an honor that pays fairly or a drain on your time with no additional compensation. Find out the rules and the pay before you agree to be a faculty lead. Often it requires numerous extra duties for limited pay; however, the trade-off is that you typically get the first section of the course, which can ultimately increase your earnings potential with greater job security.
- *Heavy discussion boards.* Mandated heavy discussion board entries can often be the largest drain on your time. Moderating a discussion by posting a comment here or there to keep things on track is great, but some schools require you to comment on everyone's responses as well as to comment on everyone's comment on a classmate's response, and the thread grows exponentially as the weeks go by. If students' grades are affected by the number of postings, and they must post three times per week, just do the math: 15 learners, each posting a response, and each posting three comments to other learners, and you must comment to each of these as well as to all replies to your own postings. To make it worse, you may have to grade their responses individually by going to the grade book and assigning individual scores with comments on why they got the grades they did.

    The focus should be on teaching, not grading. Discussions are often the lifeblood of an online course, and here is where you typically find either the greatest drain on your time or the place where a little effort goes a long way and makes you look like a great instructor.
- *Modification.* Some universities let you have free rein to modify courses as you see fit. You can modify them so students are happier

and you are less overworked on menial tasks and can focus on what's important—learner interaction. Universities that allow this level of freedom are a good thing. At first it may seem like more work, but this freedom used wisely is great in the long run and will ultimately save you time. On the flip side, some schools force adjuncts to teach from master course templates (often without allowing for any modification whatever). If this design is good for you and works with your style, then you are set; if the design is contrary to your style, you will find it more challenging to teach the course, and a waste of time when you have to readjust the course each semester. Find out if the school will replicate your particular course, not the master.

Note that if you are offered the opportunity to develop a course, you get to do it your way and then there is no need to worry about which template is used; additionally, you can often ask for the right of first refusal. Even if the pay for course development isn't great, the perks can be, so check it all out before you accept such a contract. The best deal you can get is to develop a course you have already developed at another school; it takes little time to create a similar one, and if you use the same book and same general layout, you can teach the same course at multiple schools and relax.

- *Chats.* A few universities require adjuncts to host one or more chats each week, usually by phone conference or using a system like Elluminate. This means having to type or speak a discussion with students for an hour that can be totally unproductive and completely inconvenient for you and the students. You may even have to assign grades for participation on these chats, which further intensifies the workload. In rare cases, a chat can be a time-saver, though, so don't judge too quickly.
- *Group Work.* If a course requires group work, you may find yourself assigning students to teams often and having to play referee. Sometimes, like for large papers, this is a blessing—less typing, less grading, and often better products. Other times, though, you have to set

171

up additional discussion forums and moderate them separately, which can increase your workload incredibly. If you must use groups, try to limit them to teams of two or three and you will eliminate the need for creating group areas since they can just e-mail each other easily. Also, if possible, allow students the option to work alone so as to eliminate the need to play referee.

- *Automated grading.* The more automated the grading, the better your life will be. If your course has objective exams, your only responsibility may be to create them the first time and monitor them for troublesome or unfair questions or students who get locked out for various reasons. The other added benefit is that learners get immediate feedback on objective exams, and it takes the pressure off you to grade quickly. Essays are not automatically graded, so you should keep these to a minimum, but at the graduate level it is more appropriate to have more writing and fewer objective exams, so you will need to space out these exams and assignments.

- *Submitting grades.* Some schools use grading forms you have to mail in. This means (1) you have to actually be at your home office to send in grades (or have carried the paperwork with you) and (2) it's slower. Online grading is more efficient and will make you feel as though you've truly closed a class when it's over. You also know that the grades are submitted correctly and on time, thus saving you more time and trouble. Having to mail in grading forms is not a reason to turn away a teaching opportunity, but it is something to take into account.

- *Multiple Courses.* Teaching multiple courses at the same school will naturally earn you more money, but if you teach multiple sections of the same course, it will feel like *easy* money. Two identical sections do not take double the time since you are grading the same papers and posting the same questions and assignments; the only difference may be in the flow of the discussions, but you can often use some comments from one discussion to seed the other if needed. Note, depending on how a school pays, you should consider this carefully. If a school pays by the student, a class of 20 is better than two classes of 10, but if the school pays by the class, then you want as many small sections as you can get. The key is to balance time with earnings.

Once you have evaluated the workload factors at your chosen school and considered the pay you will be earning, put the school in the matrix shown in Table 9.1. As you begin to work for universities, categorize them to help you in initially determining where to focus your efforts. You may choose to construct your own matrix that also takes into account how satisfied you are working for that particular school. Sometimes having a great boss but receiving low pay can keep good faculty at a school for years.

There is another component here: how happy you are with the school ethics. It would eat us both up to teach in a program that challenged our value systems, even if it fits in the high pay/light workload category. This is the wild card. Try to imagine a school asking you to give out a lot of Fs so that students have to take your course again, thereby generating more money for the school and more teaching opportunities for yourself; could you really work there even if it is easy money? This is between you and your conscience. Be aware, however, that there are schools that have rigorous application processes, enjoy high enrollments, and seem to play by the rules when in fact they have hidden agendas.

Table 9.1 **Time Matrix—Pay versus Workload**

	Heavy Workload	**Light Workload**
High Pay	*Not a bad position, but you can handle only so many of these.*	*Ideal position.*
Low Pay	*Try to avoid these schools.*	*Not a bad position, but you can handle only so many of these, too.*

You may not learn about the school's questionable ethics until grades are in, so don't be surprised if you find yourself teaching only one course at a school and not returning. When you find one that works with your conscience, you can stay there for a long time. It is just the initial semester that is a trial period with much time invested in application, training, course setup, and teaching, and one hopes it is a good fit for you so you can maximize the return on your investment. The more homework you do up front by networking and asking others about different schools, the less likely you will regret your decision.

Three University Situations

We've created three situations for you to look at. One is the "Absolute Ideal Situation," one is the "Tolerable and Acceptable Situation," and one is the "Cut and Run Situation." We will name these schools Great to Work for You U, I Can Live with You U, and Not on Your Life U.

In Great to Work for You U, your position and your work are highly respected. The chairs and management believe that learner expectations and learner reviews are critical to your success and put some weight in them, but also understand once in a while a few bad reviews will pop up due to someone receiving a deserved low grade. The pay is good or high, the workload is average, many of the systems (like attendance tracking) are automated, and the system the school uses to manage its online courses is exceptional. Communication is somewhat frequent but by e-mail primarily, and you are paid for anything you do that's above and beyond teaching. You have an opportunity to take on more, like faculty lead or mentoring, but you're fairly compensated for it and you are relatively in charge of the process. The school will get your input before changing course design or even textbooks on a class you routinely teach. You regularly get work and new contracts because your hard work and dedication are rewarded. Great to Work for You U is ethically sound, responsible to the community, and overall a pleasure to work for. Since turnover at these schools is incredibly low, as you might expect, you should hang on to these places for dear life if you find yourself in their faculty rotations. Even if they go through some unpleasant transitions, deal with them professionally and you won't be sorry.

I Can Live with You U respects your position and may value your contribution a number of ways, which includes student reviews, but may also be concerned with how well you play politically. Playing politically online is really tough (remember, you don't get to see these people, and your actions online are permanently stored and viewed by people you might not trust). There are some automated processes, the classroom software is all right, and you're decently compensated for work you do above and beyond. Contracts may be spotty, receiving one during one term but nothing for a while. Communication may be often and by phone, taking up a lot of your valuable time. This school may routinely increase course size, but not compensate you additionally for it. I Can Live with You U is usually ethically sound, they care about the students and the community, and overall you enjoy what you do for the school. It isn't quite a Great to Work for You U, but is a good staple school to help increase your income and maintain stability. These schools are where you will find yourself most of the time if you follow our leads. They are common, and if you do your job well enough and become the go-to person in your department, the environment can almost seem like Great to Work for You U from your perspective.

Not on Your Life U may have some of the following characteristics: They may phone you the night before a class starts, asking you to build the class that night and teach it in the morning. You may even be compensated well (they will have to when they ask you to do this!) but it isn't because they want to or because they value you; it's because they procrastinated. They routinely change textbooks one or two days before a course begins, leaving the learner and the faculty frantically updating and ordering new texts. They may sometimes be ethically sound, but appear more interested in tuition than learners' success. Their contracts may be spotty at best, or they may routinely ask you to work for them. Their system of accountability is awful: You will be accountable to someone who is hired to do nothing but check in on classrooms. You may have an opportunity to develop

175

courses but often for little pay and with tremendous rigidity. They may not even use a real course room system, but may try to pass something like a newsreader off as a course. They check their community awareness and desire to do good at the door when they come to work in the morning, and they treat adjuncts as mere contractors who add no value and are easily replaceable. While they may not fit the definition of a diploma mill, they will almost feel like one. Staying at one of these schools is like hanging on to a technology stock after the dot-com/dot-bomb crash of 2000; it will take a lot to make up for what you have already lost in time and opportunity cost before these places are profitable. So dump them and cut your losses.

Communication Is Key

Regardless of what school you teach for, what platform it is running, or how well (or poorly) it pays, chances are you are being measured and evaluated on your communication. Many of these schools do not have a formal review process.

There are several keys to good communication. First and foremost, it must be fast. Chapter 10, the technology chapter, addresses ways in which you can accomplish that. You need to be quick on the draw and not let an e-mail sit in the in-box for days before responding. Sometimes you literally have a day to respond to a contract offer. If you don't like the phone, be really, really good at e-mail. If you don't like e-mail, don't teach online! In all seriousness, most of the business you will conduct when teaching as an online facilitator will take place by e-mail. Often no news is good news; you won't hear from your chair or dean for months. This is usually a good thing, but it's a good idea to remind them you exist.

Second, do not ever, ever take part in group gripe. This is occurring at a university right now regarding lowering of pay for some faculty and increasing pay for others. The gripers are copying everyone (faculty and dean included), and making themselves look really bad. This is *not* the way to remind your bosses you exist. Use the "reply all" option with caution or only when directed. If you don't like how things are going, either deal with it, discuss it privately with your boss, or leave.

Next, always respond promptly; the same day is usually not only expected but required. Even if your bosses take weeks to respond back, you shouldn't and you really mustn't. Waiting too long to respond may cause your manager to assume you also take weeks to respond to learners, which is not a good impression for your bosses to have. Plus, you need to be in the habit of immediate responses. Your students will demand it; and trust us, if you don't respond right away they will be calling you at home or on your cell phone because they are anxious. It's part of your job to reduce their anxiety and to avoid phone calls whenever possible.

It's also important to note here that in many instances academic records require written documentation, and phone calls don't count. If you do phone a student, keep a log. This is imperative in case of any discrepancy or dispute later. Simply put, use your e-mail. Find a good filing system in a good e-mail program and be very, very organized. Respond immediately, and keep your in-box clear so you know what's new and what needs a response.

If you are lucky enough to work for a boss who rarely pings you for anything, you will need to find creative ways to let your existence be known somewhat frequently. This will help ensure you are assigned courses and that your name is fresh in their minds when they are looking for course developers or course revisers. Some ways to send e-mails to your management without looking like you're vying for attention might be:

- Tell them of a new accomplishment, and ask them to add it to your faculty profile. Add a quick note explaining the benefit this brings to your learners.
- Update your profile, name, address, and so on.
- Create a web site for your teaching material and update your profile with that information as well. This will show your dedication to the teaching profession and serve as a great resource to send your students to.

- Send an interesting article about online teaching strategy that your boss may wish to share with other faculty. Keep these e-mails brief, and use attachments for the articles in PDF or RTF format so they can be read by most individuals.
- Create an e-mail indicating how well your course is going (assuming it is—don't be dishonest), and that you'd like to suggest some revisions for the future. Bullet-point these revisions. Ask the department chairperson in a nonaggressive tone to be sure the faculty lead is aware of these. If you are lucky, the faculty lead isn't doing his or her job, and you'll take over. The best way to gain status is to earn it; if you do a great job and your department chair or dean finds you highly reliable, you will be positioned for success.
- Discuss an idea for a new course. Perhaps you work in IT, and IT for Homeland Security is a hot topic. Write up a quick description and note that you feel the program would benefit from such a course. You may add that you have the expertise to assist in development should management wish to undertake the endeavor. If you develop the course, you typically get to teach the first section each semester, and will get paid whenever the course needs updating. What a way to generate income doing what you love!

You will find other creative ways to remind your bosses that you exist, and you need to do so at least quarterly. Again, think of them as your client base and yourself as an entrepreneur. How would you remind your clients that you're out there and willing and ready to serve?

Continuously Do What Comes Easily and What You're Good At

A key to being a really good online adjunct faculty is continuously doing what you're good at. This means you need to look inside yourself and figure out what aspect of online teaching suits you best. For example, you may be really good at organizing your class schedule.

Once you figure out what you are good at, stay good at it. Even when you are tired and don't feel like answering your e-mail, do it. This will help guarantee your place in line to teach classes when the time comes. You will be known as the person the schools can count on. With many things on their plates, deans and chairpersons don't like worrying about whether tasks are being accomplished, and even the lowest person on the totem pole reports up to the higher powers when things aren't getting done. You can get a bad rap or a good rap very quickly in the world of online teaching.

Using E-Mail—Not the Phone!

This point may be driven home here more than in most books, because it is extremely important. No one wants to send an e-mail to someone only to receive a return phone call back. It's annoying; usually there is a reason an e-mail was sent in the first place. Perhaps it's their organizational method or perhaps they are using it to track what has been done and what hasn't. Perhaps they are evaluating your responsiveness. Use e-mail, not the phone, unless your boss phones you and asks you to call him or her back (or unless you need to discuss matters that you wouldn't want accidentally forwarded, such as a delicate matter regarding another faculty member). You will quickly learn the preference of each of your bosses, and then you should follow suit; in general, though, use e-mail and be prompt about it.

If you are a frequent traveler and don't like being tied to your phone, this preference for e-mail will come as a pleasant though life-altering surprise. Your students may phone you, and it's wise to return their phone calls. However, you should always encourage them in the syllabus and in your contact information to use e-mail and not the phone. There are plenty of books out there telling you how to teach, so we will save that for our colleagues, but do be mindful of others' time and be respectful by honoring the online methodology.

Life as an Adjunct—Balancing Work and Home

Balancing life as an adjunct is easier said than done. As with most home-based businesses, the line can easily be blurred between home and work, and at times it can be frustrating and feel overwhelming. When your office is upstairs, it's easy to let family or personal time suddenly be work time; the benefit is that the opposite also holds true.

There are many keys to making this work/life balance work. Some tips are:

- *Create a work space that is just that—a work space.* This should not be your child's playroom or your kitchen; it needs to be a quiet space for you to type, work, write, and address questions. It should have a conference phone and all of your equipment close by.

- *Schedule your time.* One method Dr. Babb uses to survive teaching at so many schools is to use her PDA to actually schedule in time that she is to do things. For instance, her schedule might say, "10 to 11 School X, 12 to 1 School Y" and so forth. If she finishes early, great. If not, she has allocated adequate time to handle her tasks, including submitting attendance, entering grades, and so forth. Be sure to track everything that has to be submitted and when. As you juggle multiple schools, you'll also be juggling multiple deadlines and universities that have various start and end dates. Without serious organization, it can quickly become a nightmare.

- *Remember that work time is work time, and personal time is personal time.* It might be tempting to check your e-mail again at midnight, but a key to working as an adjunct is to create office hours and stick to them. It is easy to feel as though teaching is your life, and it can quite literally take over your world. Since you'll be self-employed, you'll have to set your own boundaries and work schedule, which can be tough to adapt to, particularly if you're used to a rigid workplace.

- *Try to take at least one day off each week.* Many schools require six-day-per-week logins, which means you work six days every week without fail. You're lucky if you work for a school that gives you a holiday off; most don't. Kiss holidays and nonworking vacations good-bye! The good news is that you can be anywhere and still work; the bad news is that you must still work everywhere. Try to schedule your time so that you get one consistent day off per week.

- *Work the hours that suit you best.* Dr. Mirabella has an infant at home and chooses to spend quality time with him. Except for checking e-mails throughout the day, attending scheduled conference calls, and answering calls from students or school personnel, he spends the day being a dad. When the baby naps for two hours, he goes through all of his courses and maximizes his productivity. When the baby goes to sleep for the night, he begins again, putting in an additional six hours. One of the great advantages of the asynchronous online world is that you can work any hours you choose. You can take trips at will, as long as you are willing to take your laptop. What is important is that you decide what you value most and keep that in mind as you schedule your work and your time. Don't take on more classes than you can handle, and don't take on so many that you have no time for yourself or your family. Remember that you can make plenty of money and still have a life.

- *Above all else, have fun!* If you are not having fun as an adjunct professor, then stop making yourself, your family, and your students miserable and bail out. This is not a get-rich-quick scheme. It is a new career opportunity that has both intrinsic and extrinsic rewards, but it isn't for everyone. Some people love this job purely for the schedule, others for the freedom to work independently, others for the opportunity to put their education to fine use, and still others for the ability to make extra money during off hours. To make this your only source of income, it truly helps if you enjoy teaching and you are good at it.

10

Must-Have Technologies

Education is not preparation for life; education is life itself.
—John Dewey

Teaching online is exactly what it sounds like: an online job. As with many online jobs, there are essentials and nonessentials, and one of the essentials is technology—lots of it! Technology not only is required to actually do the job, but much of it is required to keep your hectic life organized while meeting many demanding deadlines, scheduling conference calls, and reminding yourself of important to-do items.

Much of the technological advice in this chapter is coming from Dr. Babb, who has been a technologist for years and has her PhD in information technology. The teaching advice and application are coming from both of us; we agree on the technology used from a teaching and experience point of view, regardless of your level of expertise. At the end of each section Dr. Babb gives her expert opinion on what she feels is the best solution. None of these ideas are expensive and most are not complicated (but some may require that you have a little more technical savvy or that you have a friend who can help you get there). Online auctions sites, such as eBay, may be an excellent avenue for purchasing the recommended equipment, but it helps to know what you are buying. The payoff for implementing these ideas is immeasurable, but the most important task is first to get hired; so get what you need to do the job, then get the job, and then get what you need to do the job better so you can maximize your earnings! Let's begin with what you absolutely must have to do your job. That, after all, is most important.

Internet Access

When it comes to Internet access, speed isn't everything; it's the only thing. Don't even think about using a dial-up phone modem if you expect to be an online faculty member. You cannot afford to waste time uploading files, downloading files, and opening web sites when that time could be put to more practical use. The extra cost of high-speed Internet access in your home will easily pay for itself if you teach just one online course per year. Some schools will reimburse you for it, so it wouldn't hurt to ask the trainers about this during your training. Also, the cost of having high-speed Internet access is tax-deductible if you are earning income as an online professor.

There are a few excellent options available for home use. Clear Wire picks up Internet signals and transmits them wirelessly to a router in your home. As long as it has power, you can pick up the signal on the road, too. With a good signal, you can transmit about one megabit (1 Mb) per second, about 25 times as much as the 56 kilobits (Kb) per second transmitted by a dial-up phone modem. Digital subscriber line (DSL) technology is available with many local phone companies, and is carried directly over your phone line. Often you can get a package deal with your phone company to include DSL for Internet as well as cable television. A good DSL signal can transmit about 1.5 Mb per second, about 30 times as much as a dial-up modem. The best option is clearly broadband cable; the signal is generally more stable and you can expect speeds of up to 30 Mb per second, over 500 times as much as a modem, and 20 times as much as DSL.

EXPERT TIP: The big deal here with regard to Internet access is that, in most home use cases, download speed is what is important. DSL competes in this market space well. However, with online teaching, you will find yourself uploading nearly as often as downloading, so we recommend cable setups. Try not to skimp here; not every service is available in every home, but you will get value for your investment if you get the fastest access possible for your location. So do your homework and feel the need for speed. Four megabits (4 Mb) per second or more should be adequate, provided that it is both upload and download speed.

Computers

Now you have high-speed Internet access, but you need something to access it with. Of all the equipment in your home office, the most critical is the computer, and it needs to be a fast one. This means your computer must be able to take full advantage of the high-speed Internet access and must be capable of multitasking well enough that you aren't frustrated, nor are you waiting for your machine to catch up while you have 10 Web browsers open and your e-mail up constantly. This is one case where the speed of your computer truly will make an impact on how fast you are capable of doing your work. There are many components in a computer, as you know if you've ever opened one. Every one of them contributes to speed in some way. The speed of the computer's central processing unit (CPU) is measured in gigahertz (GHz) unless your computer is really old—then it's (MHz)—with higher numbers indicating higher speed. If you buy one of the slowest on the market just to save money, you are buying trouble; you will find that it is incapable of keeping up with the programs you install. You will need plenty of memory, at least 512 megabytes; but 2 gigabytes is preferred and recommended. If you intend to have multiple windows and applications open, you'll find your memory is used up quickly and your computer begins using what is known as virtual memory. Virtual memory is hard disk space that is used as temporary memory, so it's extremely slow. Memory has speed, too, so get fast memory. Be sure you have a motherboard that supports cache memory, and get plenty of it. This also makes a big difference when it comes to speed.

Some of you may choose to work off a laptop computer, while others may prefer a desktop. Whichever is your preference must also be very reliable. You cannot afford to have your computer crash or be bogged down with software you don't need. If you are not computer savvy, you might want to invest in a service where you get 24/7 technical support. For desktop computers, stay away from any name-brand computers and have a clone built at a local computer store (unless you know how to do it yourself), which is cheaper and often as reliable as or more reliable than name brands (think of it like the generic products in the grocery store for which you pay less because their packaging and marketing costs are less). Also, it won't come with a bunch of software installed that bogs down your computer. If you are like most people and don't have a lot of computer knowledge, then buy a brand name, but format the hard drive when you get it and start over, reinstalling the operating system and the software you need. We know that it sounds like a lot of trouble—and in fact it is. But you can easily speed a machine up 25 percent to 50 percent simply by starting from scratch and installing only the software you want or need versus the junk software that manufacturers typically install.

To help maintain reliability, there are certain programs every computer needs, which will be addressed later in the chapter. You must also try to implement certain practices to minimize problems; if possible, download and test potentially unusable or unneeded software on another machine, not the one you teach on. Consider your teaching personal computer (PC) your production server for business; no testing is ever done in a production server in a reputable IT shop. It's done in the test environment or what we call the "sand box" before it is transferred to production.

It's amazing what using a download site can do to your PC when you install a free tool that tracks your every move as part of its free use agreement. You may not have the luxury of a second computer, but if you plan to teach online more than just as a hobby, it is worth the investment in a second computer, which doesn't have to be new or even top-of-the-line.

You should also consider having a laptop even if you prefer to work off a desktop. Even with the best computer equipment, you cannot control how often the Internet may go down in your home. Short of a hurricane that wipes out power in your city, there is no reason you cannot take your laptop to the nearest coffee shop and continue to do your course work. Plus there is the added benefit of being able to take a trip while working on your laptop to keep up with your classes. A laptop is good not only for backups but because once you get on a speaking circuit and you are visiting residencies and traveling with your newfound freedom, you will need to be able to teach remotely. Name brands are fine here, but get something fast. Don't skimp on the processor or memory to save a few hundred bucks.

EXPERT TIP: Your PC should support at least a Pentium 4 and be at least a 2 gigabyte processor with half a gigabyte of memory or more, and the motherboard should support cache memory. It's okay to buy a non-name-brand motherboard, but don't do the same for your processor. Of all the name brands Dell is the most reliable desktop and Sony is the most reliable laptop. This is our conclusion after seeing and using nearly all kinds and watching what needed repair, what stopped working at random, and what users had the most trouble with. If you want to buy a clone, go to a computer store and ask the staff to build you a custom one, or buy the parts and do it yourself if you know how.

Backups

Backups are the second most critical item next to Internet access that you will need for your computer. You absolutely must have backups. Some online systems store student grades on their systems; others don't and you must keep spreadsheets and records. You can buy a second PC and have the company you use install Windows Server (any of the versions will work fine), which looks and acts relatively the same as Windows. Local network or computer experts can come set up your server. This is not nearly as difficult as it sounds. After it's installed, you can back data up to it, and if you want to get savvy you can even run other server-based applications from it. Other solutions include backing up to a remote server (there are many services you can buy to do this) or simply moving data perhaps from a desktop to a laptop weekly. The key here is consistency and making certain you have at least one copy off-site in case someone steals your computers. Make sure your backups are working and make sure you do them often. Online backups allow you to store your data on someone else's server and pay for the service. This does make recovering easier, and is especially useful if you actually lose your computer due to fire or theft. DataSafe, MCI, McAfee, and Connected Online Backup are four examples of companies that offer this service. You should also set whatever software or service you decide to use up to auto-backup your data; you can download free software to do this at CNET's Download.com (www.download.com). This will save you tremendous headaches should something become corrupted; you won't get hit with a virus, or worse.

Also, if your PC is down, you won't have time to get it up and running before teaching again. Students will be waiting; you'll need to take your laptop to a local coffee shop and get working, then come home and fix up your machine. If you have off-site backups, you can pull data from anywhere you have Internet access. Ideally if you set your PC to automatically back up to the Internet nightly, your risk of losing files is minimized.

EXPERT TIP: One option you have is to back up to a local or a remote server or computer; this could be another computer at your home, a server at your home, or a remote server elsewhere. You need to mitigate several types of risks depending on where you live: fire, theft, and also corruption. So based on those criteria, decide whether you need off-site backups before making your decision. One option is to buy another hard drive, copy the data to it, and store it at a friend's house. The trouble there is that you'll need to do this at the very minimum every week; ideally you would do it every night. If you use your laptop as your backup device, recovery is far faster and you can easily move from your desktop to your laptop with little hassle, but you won't have the benefit of reducing fire or theft data loss risk. Ideally, though, you would pay for a service and back up to the Internet nightly what's changed (called an incremental backup) and weekly all files (a full backup). New services are being introduced regularly and for amazingly cheap prices offering encrypted transmission. Do searches in your favorite search engine to find the latest and greatest.

Organization Systems and PDAs

It doesn't matter whether you use Outlook, a Palm application, or some off-the-wall product you got free online, but use something to remind yourself when to submit attendance at certain schools, when various programs start, when to set up new classes, when to e-mail your bosses, and various other recurring tasks. Make sure you can schedule recurring appointments, and if you can categorize, it will make doing so even easier.

Now, this brings up yet another requirement. Whatever you choose, it *must* synchronize to a PDA. This can be a Treo (which will let you get e-mail, too), a Windows-based device like an iPAQ from Hewlett-Packard (HP), a Palm that doesn't get e-mail—whatever you choose. However, it's recommended that if you're on the road a lot and consulting, too, that you seriously consider a device that lets you get e-mail remotely so that your students (and bosses) aren't left hanging waiting for your reply e-mail. This is particularly true if you still have a day job and you're checking your e-mail from work (watch out—many consider this a conflict of interest).

EXPERT TIP: If you decide to make a transition to more seamlessly receive e-mail remotely, you will need to save your data, do a lot of legwork up front, and find a good solution that fits your needs. Do your homework and your transition will be far less stressful. You won't want to do this twice! If you are all about speed and simplicity and don't necessarily need off-site e-mail, stick with a Palm. If the speed with which you can do things is not so important and e-mail is, then go with a Windows CE device. Windows CE will also run other Microsoft applications rather seamlessly.

189

Newsgroup Software

Some schools use newsgroups to manage and run their courses instead of Web-based systems. There are very few out there, but the largest online school in the country happens to use newsgroups. Most faculty members we know don't like this system as it's cumbersome and very time-consuming; however, to teach for these schools you must adopt their standards, or at least be willing to tolerate them.

Outlook Express comes inherently with a newsgroup reader; Outlook itself does not. However, if you use Outlook for calendaring and e-mail you may not want to also use Outlook Express; it's tough enough dealing with so many login IDs and sites, much less two e-mail systems. You also can't synchronize these newsgroups with your PDA if you use Outlook Express, but Outlook doesn't support newsgroups. Look for other software available online that creates integration between the standard Outlook version and newsgroups, letting you log in to newsgroups from Outlook, which you cannot do without added software. This will keep you from having to check multiple accounts, unless of course you use Outlook Express for your e-mail anyway.

EXPERT TIP: Simon Smith's software is inexpensive (less than $10) and works well to create integration between Outlook and newsgroups, not to mention that he provides the best support anyone could ask for. Check out his software at www.ghytred.com/NewsLook. You can't get better support, nor can you find a better piece of software out there. Dr. Babb has personally tested his latest version and she endorses it emphatically.

Cellular Phones

Most schools require office hours. Unless you want to sit by your phone all day, get a cell phone with a lot of minutes and the ability to reach international numbers if you teach students in other countries. Chances are you'll want to take student calls on the run and you will be required to check voice mail while on vacations. Be sure to have some sort of headset for traveling and for home. It will save your shoulders and keep you safer on the road.

EXPERT TIP: Don't have your PDA and your cell phone on the same device! As nice as this level of integration sounds if you carry around a small purse, it isn't. You may want to be on the phone while looking things up; also, the PDA phones are clumsy and difficult to use as phones. No one device is excellent at both. Dr. Babb prefers Samsung phones due to their quality and ease of use, and HP for Windows CE devices. Each device does what it does best. Stick with a cell phone for phone calls and a PDA for organizing. In the long run, you'll probably be very happy with this combination.

Voice-Over Internet Protocol (VoIP)

Although VoIP may be a nice to have, it still suffers from quality of service issues in many areas and can make things complicated. Still, Dr. Babb uses Skype on occasion and is content with the quality. Companies like Vonage will save you money, but the sound quality isn't so great. We've been on conference calls with individuals using Vonage, and you can tell they're not on a fast enough broadband system. After hearing of a recent issue with Vonage and faxing and doing a little research, we concluded that it is well documented that using fax machines over Vonage systems doesn't always work, so you are really limiting yourself. Pay for an inexpensive online faxing service, use Skype and your cell phone, and you won't even have reason to have a home phone!

EXPERT TIP: Don't use VoIP unless you have excellent broadband service, or you won't be happy. Corporate VoIP systems rely on an industry-wide initiative called Quality of Service (QoS), and QoS components and applications are impossible to route over the Internet. Since corporations have dedicated lines between offices in most cases, they can successfully use VoIP services because they can guarantee that voice packages will have priority on the network over other packets. What this means to the end user is that at home, your voice calls won't sound that great without a really high-speed network, despite what the commercials say. You may not notice, but the person on the other end will. Don't pay for these services when there are many that are free and more are popping up every day. You can even download a version of Skype to run on your PDA!

Unified Messaging

Whereas some might consider this a nice thing to have, Dr. Babb considers it a requirement. Unified messaging is a system that dumps voice mail into your e-mail. This allows you several advantages: (1) if you are traveling out of the country, you can forward your cell phone to the unified messaging system and still check your voice mail and not miss messages; (2) you can retain your privacy and not give out your cell number unless for emergencies; (3) it's nice to have everything in one system, particularly letting you forward or reply to voice messages in standard .wav or other formats to other individuals. One that Dr. Babb is particularly fond of is called K7.net (online at www.k7.net). While the free service gives you a Denver-based phone number, the system is amazing and reliable. You can pay for a local number or even a toll-free number.

EXPERT TIP: Always ask callers to leave their e-mail address so you can respond to them by e-mail if you prefer. This saves headaches if you're out of the country. The system automatically records the number the caller is calling from and puts it in the subject of the message (unless it's a blocked number) so if you do need to call back, you will know the number without having to listen to the entire message. K7.net is truly an amazing service and is highly recommended. It also helps you stay a bit more anonymous if you're a little uncomfortable about certain students having your personal information, which will happen from time to time.

Comfortable and Ergonomic Workstation Setups

You will be on your computer a lot. Have a comfortable, ergonomic workstation environment and save your wrists and hands. Dr. Babb recommends natural keyboards; you can even purchase natural mice now depending on the size of your hand. Check out the numerous ergonomic sites and be sure you are comfortable.

EXPERT TIP: Dr. Babb brought in an ergonomic specialist to take pictures of her typing after having difficulty with posture and pain from being on her computer all day. For $325, she got a thorough evaluation, her workstation measured, and everything adjusted well. It definitely saved a lot of trouble.

Conference Phones

If you intend to take calls from home, consider an inexpensive solution from a company like Polycom for a small conferencing system or a voice conference system from your favorite VoIP provider. This will allow you clear, office-quality conference calls for far less money.

EXPERT TIP: Dr. Babb got hers on eBay for a fraction of retail: under $200. It's the PolyCom Voice Station 100 and works incredibly well.

Instant Messaging

One option to consider for allowing your students to get hold of you is instant messaging (IM). You can use any of several systems, including America Online (AOL) or Microsoft (MSN). Having one will help you keep people from phoning. Some find the instant messaging more annoying than phone calls, though, so this is your call.

EXPERT TIP: Using a system like Trillian will let you have one IM application but several IM addresses. This is important if you want to keep it simple but offer multiple solutions for your learners. Sometimes learners will want to use IM to get hold of you, but they are using AOL's Instant Messenger and you are using MSN Messenger. While they are not incompatible, receiving messages from both means you have to have two login IDs and two systems running all of the time. This type of system (and there are several out there for free) will let you use one software solution to log in to all of your accounts. Organize the contacts that send you messages by school as they come in (ask them to tell you what school they are with), so that in the future you'll know right away which group they belong to and you can more easily answer their questions without looking like you're juggling classes.

Fax—Electronic and Traditional

Electronic faxes will allow you to send and receive faxes by e-mail and via a Web interface. This is incredibly convenient, especially when traveling. In addition, moving is a breeze; your numbers don't change! Traditional fax machines act as copiers and also let you send out quickly, another consideration. Dr. Babb uses both; she has a traditional fax machine for sending and receiving large files or contracts unrelated to teaching, and she has her Myfax account for smaller teaching-related faxes. Either way, you'll need to fax contracts to schools and even sometimes copies of textbook pages to students who might find that a page is missing from their text. Add this capability to your home office.

EXPERT TIP: Dr. Babb likes Myfax and EFax, both inexpensive and quality services online. She has used both, and actually prefers the lesser-known MyFax due to the quality of the faxes and the ease of the system; it's also relatively low-priced. However, there appears to be no way to automatically resend faxes that don't go through or to have MyFax automatically retry. This is a flaw in the faxing system or a feature that users aren't readily aware of. If you do a lot of outbound faxing, EFax might be better for you. It offers free accounts, but limits the number of incoming pages before cutting off your free account; it's not very convenient but good for a trial period.

PDF Converters

Adobe's Portable Document Format (PDF) has become the de facto standard for sharing documents and information. Even official documents are being sent online this way. PDFs are less difficult to tamper with than Word or Excel documents, for instance, and most people are able to view them on their equipment. PDF readers are free online, and most universities will share information this way. A PDF converter lets you take, for instance, a Word file and save it as a PDF file, and vice versa. This lets you manipulate PDF files to sign contracts and easily send them back; it also lets you save, for instance, a Word test file into a PDF that students can't copy and paste from. This software has a multitude of uses and is relatively inexpensive.

EXPERT TIP: PDF-Pro from ePapyrus is one that Dr. Babb likes and uses often, but there are many others. If you search through Download.com you will find many other options as well. PDF files can get quite large, so students without high-speed Internet access have trouble with them and you won't be able to upload them without a system that provides for fast uploads. See the Internet access section earlier in the chapter on what to do to solve this issue (hint: buy cable!).

Scanners

Your scanner will serve many purposes: scanning in direct deposit forms for schools, scanning transcripts to send when interviewing, or scanning articles for learners to read. A good one (Dr. Babb likes HP scanners) will serve as a scanner, fax (scans to PDF to be faxed off), and auto e-mailer (automatically e-mails a scanned file with the touch of a button).

EXPERT TIP: Invest in a good scanner and it will last you a long time. Usually legal-size files aren't a requirement unless you're also handling real estate transactions, so don't stress about finding one that handles legal-size paperwork. Many of the newer ones will do things like scan in negatives from film; decide what's important and take those things into account when making your decision. Using an automatic document feeder (ADF) will save you considerable time, particularly if you're scanning articles to share with students. This can also be used to clean out file drawers and archive what isn't so important anymore (like old tax files).

Printers

Even though you're teaching online, you'll find yourself printing student files and reading offline; so you'll want a fast printer and one that uses ink that doesn't cost a lot (we find color to be unnecessary). Find one that will use cheap paper, too, because some will jam with lightweight paper. When you're printing student papers to read on the couch, you won't want to fork over $6 for 500 sheets of paper!

EXPERT TIP: An HP fan and an IT person who has seen a lot of printers break (and many survive), Dr. Babb recommends a midquality HP laser printer. You can get these from online auctions relatively cheaply. If you are going to teach on-ground classes, consider a color ink-jet printer, as well, for handouts.

Backup Internet Providers

It might not be a bad idea to have a backup Internet provider, such as T-Mobile (it also works great when traveling), that you can use at local coffee shops if your Internet access goes down. Without Internet access you are dead in the water.

EXPERT TIP: Many cellular phone providers offer a PCMCIA laptop card to let you connect while on the road. This not only is an ultraportable solution, but it may cost less, too. Be sure to look for only high-speed options!

Uninterruptible Power Supply (UPS)

Don't run your PCs and laptops without an uninterruptible power supply (UPS). Not only will a UPS protect your equipment from power surges and lightning, but your system will continue running even in a power outage. Dr. Babb uses the American Power Conversions brand and utilizes the Smart UPS 1000 on her server and her desktop and laptop PCs. One device for the desktop and laptop will keep the equipment running on its own for about a day, with normal use, even without regular power. If you put your Internet cable modem and router on a UPS, you can have your network run well while the power is out! The investment cost is between $300 and $700, depending on which model you get, but there are many options available and it will save your equipment, keep power flow regulated (which prolongs the life of your equipment), and keep you running in an outage.

EXPERT TIP: If you want your battery to last longer, don't connect peripheral components that you don't absolutely need, like scanners and printers.

Wireless at Home

Consider using wireless at home. Note that there *is* always speed degradation between wired and wireless. Your home desktop and even your laptop, if that's your primary computer, should have a hardwired connection. Wireless lets you roam about the house, and teach while cooking dinner. D–Link makes excellent wireless routers, but so do Belkin and LinkSys. Any of those options would be good. Stay away from any product that is using a nonstandard and non–backward-compatible system, such as some of the new 802.11 standards. Until all the vendors agree on a standard for interoperability, if you adopt the standard you will have to use all of that one equipment manufacturer's components! This means the built-in wireless card in your laptop may not work. For now, stick with support of 802.11 a, b, and g.

EXPERT TIP: If you're having issues getting a signal in various parts of the house, use a system that lets you have a wireless repeater. This will cut down on problems, particularly if you have a two-story home.

Virus Protection

This is a must-have on any machine. Virus writers write destructive forces faster than we can keep up. Get a good one, pay for it, and have it auto-update its definition files daily while you're not using your computer. Let it auto-scan every morning sometime before you start work.

EXPERT TIP: Unless you are on a serious energy conservation trip, just leave your computer on and let it scan while you're sleeping. I know this makes a lot of people nervous; they have nightmares of burning down their house or sky-high electricity bills. You can just turn off your monitor but let the PC run. It has jobs to do at nighttime, particularly while the room is cool; it's better for the drives to churn away in ideal temperatures so that you don't overheat your machine.

Antispam

Spam can bog down your e-mail system, as you already know. The best solution is to turn it on from your Internet service provider (ISP) so that you don't receive junk mail at all. The trouble is, sometimes there are messages that get dumped into the spam box that shouldn't be there, so check it often and be sure to unblock domains of schools you work for. You don't want to miss important messages. A quick tip not many people realize: Spammers will usually find you because you bought something online, put in your e-mail address, or downloaded some application that tracked you.

The mass spammers also just randomize letters and send to major known providers, so having a tricky e-mail address keeps you somewhat protected from this type of spam. There is a positive correlation between surfing the Web/buying online and spam. Be careful who you submit your e-mail address to and look at their policies.

EXPERT TIP: Be careful downloading software, especially the free kind. Read the license agreements, boring as they are. If they are tracking you or installing spyware, don't use them. It's rare to get something for nothing these days. Shareware (software that is on an honor system for paying, like Simon's) often puts an annoying message like "Register me!" every two times you start it up, but it will continue working without registration. When you pay the usually small fee to register it, the messages go away. Often these individuals don't put spyware into their systems. We recommend avoiding crippleware at all costs because it will work for a while for free and then ask for payment before continuing. This is annoying and you'll be left feeling disappointed, and who knows what they installed on your PC. Anything that says it works "partially" or "is somewhat locked" should be avoided. It's a scam. Be sure to add domains for all your universities to the safe list. If you work for Northcentral University, for example, put@ncu.edu on the safe list so that systems are less likely to discard valid mail.

E-Mail Accounts with In-Box High Limits

By high limit, we don't mean a high spending limit. Some of your learners will send you enormously large files; some of your bosses will, too. At the minimum, you should be able to receive a 10 megabyte e-mail. Some systems, like Hotmail, will let you pay a small premium and receive 25 megabyte e-mails. In addition, your total available mailbox limit should be at least 2 gigabytes, or you should walk. Hotmail offers this, as does Google's Gmail, and Google is free (some versions of Hotmail are, too). Check around but don't settle for a 100 megabyte e-mail in-box! Not only will your senders be frustrated, but you will be, too. You should know Hotmail is devising some great new products that will allow you to remotely retrieve your calendar and synchronize your PDA with Hotmail. Check into it and watch for these new upcoming versions of software.

EXPERT TIP: You can have all your e-mail come into Outlook or Outlook Express to avoid checking each school's Web mail system. However, we must caution you that schools usually require you to use their servers. This means you need to have both the Post Office Protocol, (POP3, incoming) and Simple Mail Transfer Protocol (SMTP, outgoing) mail addresses for their servers, if possible, or use your own local ISP for the SMTP address; however, you must be sure to send out through the account the mail came in on. This way the university has the e-mail coming from their school, yet you're using your own system. You will be asked to keep e-mail on each of the mail systems; this is one way to avoid having to log in to Web mail. This does not keep a copy on the university's system, though, so in some way you're circumventing its process. This method is usually okay, but be sure to save copies of everything in case you're asked for them at universities that require you to use their mail systems. Also, it's advisable to let your bosses know you are doing this. Tell them you are using their inbound and outbound servers, but storing mail on your local PC; usually you won't run into any trouble. Students also need to think the e-mail came from the domain they sent it to so they don't receive an e-mail from Northcentral University when they sent it to Walden. Remember you work for each school independently.

Professional Web Sites

A web presence gives you credibility and allows you to expand your reach. It gives you a platform by which you can give resources to students, show your bio to potential universities you want to work for, and demonstrates that you take the job seriously. This helps make you real to your online world, something that is tough to do sometimes. The more you can make yourself a real person behind a keyboard, the better off you'll be. If you choose to write a book or sell on eBay, you can also put up a link.

EXPERT TIP: Look at Dr. Mirabella's web site at www.drjim mirabella.com and Dr. Babb's at www.drdaniellebabb.com. Notice a theme with the names? Make the site name something that gives you instant credibility and is easy for your learners to remember. Your name is a good place to start, as it helps ensure you aren't using someone else's copyrighted name and guarantees that your site will be open.

Antispyware Software

Spyware will take down the best system. Spyware is software that runs in the background of your machine, doing a variety of not-so-nice things. This includes monitoring your activities and even reporting to a marketing server what you did, where you went online, and what you bought. Often it's distributed within downloadable crippleware or freeware products.

EXPERT TIP: Several solutions are out there to help you manage this nightmare. AdAware and SpyBot Search and Destroy are the two that Dr. Babb recommends. Either way, update them regularly and run them on a schedule and anytime you notice your computer slowing down.

Office Suites

By office suite, we don't mean renting an office; we mean acquiring equipment including a word processor, spreadsheet program, and presentation package. We all know that Microsoft Office dominates in this area, and most schools will use these. Be able to at least support them.

EXPERT TIP: Consider using a PDA that supports at least a reader of each of these products so that if you're checking e-mail remotely and need to answer something with an attachment, you aren't pressured into rushing back home. Any Windows CE device should come standard with pocket versions of Word, PowerPoint, and Excel.

Backup Hard Drives

You should keep at least one backup hard drive in stock, so to speak. Have a duplicate of your software on it using hard drive duplication software like Ghost. You should have the hard drive bootable and use this as a spare. A laptop drive with a 60 gigabyte drive in it connected by USB cable is an excellent way to back up data and store it off-site.

EXPERT TIP: Another option is to do this same thing on a several-gigabyte USB drive, although it's far cheaper to have two drives. USB drives can offer another advantage; you can easily travel with your data and use it on anyone else's PC, and some have built-in wireless network cards. If you buy an extra hard drive, you can mirror or duplex them, a method that allows you to bring the other drive up automatically should one fail.

Password Storage

You will be asked to remember more passwords than you ever thought imaginable in your life! This means you need a password and site storage utility. This could be something you store on your own and tape underneath your desk should your computer be stolen, or an actual tool (many are available at www.download.com) that stores this data.

EXPERT TIP: Be sure your storage utility is a safe and secure solution. They are made for PDAs also, so you could choose to store them off-site.

Software and Keys

There will be a time, at the least convenient moment, when you have to reinstall software, or even your entire operating system. You'll want either the compact discs (CDs) or the applications on a server. Dr. Babb copies the CDs to her server hard drive when she gets them along with the keys or license code so she has everything in one place and all of her computers can share software. Dr. Mirabella keeps his CDs with the latest versions of his keys.

EXPERT TIP: Keep the license codes handy even if your CDs are not. Sometimes you'll need to update something and won't have time to search for an installation CD, but will be asked for a product code. Stay away from software that requires "hard coding" or "dongles," devices that connect to your computer to authenticate you.

Minimum School Requirements Example

This section offers a glimpse into what one school requires as its minimum standard. This is from DeVry University, available publicly online at www.devry.edu/whydevry/online_options_technical_specs.jsp. This gives you an idea of what the universities expect from you; remember this is the minimum. You'll want to run the most efficient business possible, so this is not all that we recommend.

- Windows 2000, XP Home, or XP Professional.
- Microsoft Office XP Professional or higher, including Word, Excel, PowerPoint, and Access.
- A 600 MHz Pentium PC or comparable with 256 MB of RAM (512 recommended).
- Ten gigabytes of total hard disk space, or 8 GB available after the operating system (OS) installation.
- A 56 Kb model or better for dial-up (optional high-speed Internet).
- CD-ROM or DVD drive.
- ISP account for Internet access and e-mail.
- Java-enabled Web browser using Internet Explorer (IE) 5.5 or 6.0, Netscape 6.20, or Netscape Communicator 4.77. AOL is not supported.
- Flash Plug-In.
- Acrobat Reader.

- Realplayer.
- QuickTime.
- Antivirus software.
- Sound capability.
- PCs recommended; Macintosh computers may be used but in some cases are not supported.
- Screen resolution set to 800 × 600 or 1,024 × 768 recommended.

We think these minimums would not allow you to sufficiently run your course. We do not know of any online teacher who can work using a dial-up system, or who can work with only a 10 gigabyte hard drive. Most likely your own system configurations will far exceed the standard set by the university, so just keep your equipment relatively current and you'll be fine. A 600 MHz processor is easily attainable on eBay for about $10. You should have a 2 gigabyte or greater processor, at least. Also it's important to note here that there are many schools that don't support Macs. They were fairly common in universities some time ago, but are less common now.

Making Your Life Easier and the Students Happier

Most of the technologies mentioned thus far are designed for you to support your students, keep your life more organized, and make your business easier to manage. Some also help you look good to your bosses and make you more accessible. We recommend giving students many ways to contact you, but keeping it simple enough that you'll actually use them. For instance, don't offer an IM address if you are rarely at your computer. Don't offer a cell number if you don't like to answer your phone. Keep the students in mind; keep your life simple and easy, but remember that your students are often anxious and need answers right away. You have committed to responding to them promptly, and that is one area of your performance that you will be judged harshly on in evaluations. This is important, but make sure it's also doable.

Setting Up a System to Support Flexibility and Travel

When you begin life as an adjunct, you won't be traveling much. As time goes on, you will find that this schedule picks up much more dramatically, particularly if you teach in doctoral programs that have residencies. You'll want to set up a system that supports flexibility and travel. This means several things:

- Data that's easily transferable between laptop and desktop.
- An organization method that is easy to follow and keeps both computers in sync. For instance, Dr. Babb creates a "for desktop" folder on her laptop while she's traveling. When she returns, she copies everything in that folder to her desktop to make sure that the two computers are always in sync and there are no conflicting file versions out there.
- A method to access e-mail while at airports or waiting for a rental car or a bus.
- A laptop with a wireless Internet card built in.
- A straightforward, reliable laptop that is configured just like your desktop. (This includes software you will use for only one class but may need while traveling. Better to always install on both PCs than be traveling and realize you don't have what you need.)

The key here is to understand how you do things, your lifestyle, what's important to you, and how you work. Then mimic this in your technology. You will find traveling a joy and far less stressful.

11

Maintaining Relationships and Growing Your Business

None of us got where we are solely by pulling ourselves up by our bootstraps. We got here because somebody—a parent, a teacher, an Ivy League crony, or a few nuns—bent down and helped us pick up our boots.

—Thurgood Marshall

Either you've begun teaching for at least one university (or are being trained to do so), and you're on your way to a successful life as an adjunct, or you've made the life-changing decision to earn your degree and pursue this incredible life. Whether this is a transition period for you or your intended future career, you will find many rewards and opportunities in the virtual world.

As you begin your new adventure and freedom working online and have quite possibly taught or at least trained in your first course, maybe it was everything you dreamed of and more, maybe it was just an okay experience, or maybe it was more painful than a root canal. Before you either pack it in because it's not what you expected or go to the opposite extreme and quit your full-time job because you struck pay dirt, you need to reflect on your goals.

Personal Motivation

Why are you doing this? Are you teaching online so as to share the wisdom that you have gathered over the years with those who might benefit from it? Do you enjoy facilitating adult learners (this is by far your largest audience) who bring their own knowledge and expertise to the table? Are you just hoping to have stimulating discussions on your favorite subjects because you cannot do so at work or at home? Are you trying to make contacts for your full-time career in consulting or some other profession? Are you trying to repay a debt that a former teacher of yours told you that you owed for what he/she did for you? Are you in pursuit of a full-time teaching position? Are you just looking to supplement your income? Take some time to reflect on why you are doing what you're doing.

Whatever your needs and goals, ask yourself if online teaching is going to meet those needs and goals. Perhaps you've tried it but it doesn't really stimulate you or let you earn enough money for the time invested, or it doesn't give you the fulfillment you expected. Or maybe it does all of this and more. This is not a fly-by-night opportunity; it is real work, and often hard work at that, but it has incredible upsides and is one of the most fulfilling jobs imaginable. The commitment involved to make this a success is huge, for it takes a lot of effort not only to get the job, but to keep the job, too, and you cannot even think about joining this profession in a full-time capacity without first earning an accredited graduate degree.

You must have an unselfish attitude and genuinely care that others learn and that the integrity of a college degree is upheld. The respect you get from being a faculty member is unprecedented. Besides making some excellent income, the biggest thing you can make is a difference. How many jobs are there where you can feel good about what you do while actually making a living from home or while traveling? How many jobs are there where you touch so many lives at once, and people will talk of you for years to come? How many jobs are there where you are treated as an expert because of your title and where the respect is yours to lose? How many jobs are there where you will have had dozens of good and bad role models to observe firsthand for several years? We know of one such job for sure!

Keys to Successful Relationships in a Virtual World

As with any job or career you undertake, you must maintain relationships to be successful in the online world. It can be even more difficult and demanding because, unlike a more traditional workplace, you don't actually see your boss very often, if ever. As we mentioned earlier in the book, despite this difficulty, you must make yourself known and be considered present. Your bosses must know you by name and think of you when they think of various positive qualities (like responsive, student centered, a great writer, etc.), and it is your job to maintain these virtual relationships.

With the growth of online education, deans spend more time recruiting and training new faculty than they do maintaining the current ones, so it is easy to be forgotten if you are not the go-to faculty member. This is not always intentional but it does happen. Sometimes you will learn that you were deselected but never told, or that your course has been dropped from the catalog but no one bothered to find a different course for you. You may come to realize that you are better off resigning, but you will never know if you don't investigate.

So how do you maintain relationships when you never see your manager? You could just do your job and chances are your contracts will be renewed, but your workload probably won't increase. You probably won't be at the top on the list for well-paying speaking engagements, or be considered a subject matter expert. Most likely you won't be considered for development work, either. You need to be on top of your game and proactive with your work. In IT, we use the word *ping*. To ping means to hit or tap another server; according to SearchNetworking.com, "Ping is a basic Internet program that allows a user to verify that a particular IP address exists and can accept requests. . . . Loosely, ping means 'to get the attention of' or 'to check for the presence of' another party online." Ping is the best word we can find to describe what you need to do with your online managers.

In the real world, you need to ping your managers on a regular basis. If you use a PDA for scheduling, you might consider scheduling a recurring event in which you find an article of interest and send it to your managers. Don't do a mass "to" e-mail! Be sure to e-mail each person privately and indicate how you thought it might pertain to that person's school, if in fact you do. Otherwise a simple "I found this article interesting and thought I'd pass it on" is fine. In some cases a general e-mail inquiry might just get forwarded to another department chair who is looking for faculty. It's far easier to give additional classes to existing faculty than to hire.

Some other examples of e-mails you might want to send are:

Last year, I updated XYZ course. It might be time to consider another quick glance at the course because several technologies have changed. Last year when we discussed convergence in the course, we did not have the ability to segment traffic like we do today. This is one example of areas that may need updating. FYI.

Or:

Thanks for forwarding my evaluations. It's very motivating to hear of student satisfaction, and I wanted you to know how much I enjoy working for you!

Quick e-mails like this are often best, because they don't ask for anything but they do show your desire to work there and subtly reinforce the impression that students think you're doing well. "Thanks for your confidence in me. I won't let you down." is a nice reply to an e-mail from your boss letting you know your contract has been renewed. Sincerity is definitely a key here. It's okay to toot your own horn; just be sure you're also being honest and genuine in your approach.

Find your own style, but remind your bosses that you exist. Remind them of your capabilities. Remind them of other areas of interest that you have. Sometimes it doesn't pay off because you're filling a need for them in the area where you already teach, but sometimes it does. At the very least they are reminded of your existence without a mental image of you! Sending greeting cards for holidays or boss's day is entirely appropriate. Remember the administrative assistants, too. Think of them as gatekeepers; they often are. Just a simple "Thank you" e-mail to these gatekeepers will go a long way.

Fit in before you stick out! And once you do fit in, you can speak up about changes you recommend. But be careful: If you speak too soon, you may be seen as a complainer or misfit; if you speak too late after everyone sees the problems, you may be seen as a blamer who looks for reasons why things aren't working well but won't accept personal responsibility; if you time it right, you are a team player and a trusted adviser. The object is to join the team, become a vital part of the team, become a superstar, and then seek to become a team leader.

Varying Demands by University

Every university that you work for will have different demands of you, as addressed in Chapter 9. Some require weekly attendance reporting and some don't require it at all. Some require that you hold regular and posted office hours, and some don't require office hours. When you go through training, the requirements of you as a faculty member will be clearly laid out. Ask any questions you have then, because you will want to be clear when each item is due. Note it somewhere, and then if you get to teach a class with that college, find an organizational method that works for you

211

and stick with it. Remember to keep your own time demands in check, and realize that one downside to this career is that most likely schools won't take breaks at the same time. This means very little, if any, vacation for you; the last thing you want is to be burned out before you even start, and it can happen. Find ways to manage your time and create personal boundaries, such as not working past a certain time of night or not giving out your cell phone number. You will learn with time what works for you and what doesn't.

The important thing is that you clearly identify the demands placed on you, clearly note them, find an organizational method that works for you, and begin to effectively manage your time and the demands placed on you.

Keeping Everyone Happy

We have established that every university and each school within it will have particular demands. Remember that often an accreditation body governs these demands, and without this accreditation, enrollment drops and so do your teaching opportunities. You do not want to work for diploma mills and you don't want to work for universities that don't respect your position.

So, while juggling multiple positions at multiple universities, how do you keep everyone happy? For starters, set your own boundaries so you can realistically tell people what to expect. Everything you commit to must always be followed through in its entirety, whether this is a commitment to your students or to your bosses. This means your commitments need to be realistic, and not forgotten! It sounds simple enough, but when your course development manager is e-mailing you daily with course updates that need to be done, three bosses are asking questions, and you have 10 classes at six different schools, this can be quite a feat. If you fail to meet student commitments, that will quickly be noticed by the department chairpersons. Once you make a commitment, find a way to schedule it and remind yourself of it so you can work on it and beat your own deadline. Sometimes your needs and the schools' needs won't mesh and you have to make concessions.

We established the need to set personal boundaries and then set commitments on projects or deadlines. Of course this must work within the established time frame; if grades are due in seven days, you can't e-mail your boss and tell him or her to expect them in 10 days! Just pace yourself and schedule accordingly. Be very organized and diligent, and meet your commitments. Should you fail at a commitment, own up to it, take your bumps and bruises, and move on. You will be respected more than if you try to create a lame excuse. More often than not, a slipup will be overlooked if it is infrequent. If you find that meeting commitments is becoming challenging, then cut back on the commitments until you have more time or can perhaps reorganize yourself; you will be respected more for declining an opportunity than failing at one.

Next, stay in touch. We've discussed many ways you can do this. One thing department chairpersons have noted they like is feedback on the course—what students complain about (or like). Some schools do a good job of trying to get the faculty community established and maintained, but others do not. So reach out first and provide valuable information.

We have also talked about being responsive and we've discussed some technical ways you can do that. Follow through with your commitment when you decided to be responsible for a group of students learning; be responsive and take student concerns and needs seriously. This doesn't mean you need to remove personal space; just be considerate (and expect the same in return—any good boss will back you on that decision). This requires rapport, which you must build with your managers. Once you have it, you will be free to express yourself and your thoughts to your manager, within reason. Stay away, at all costs, from public venting sessions that often occur on faculty newsgroups. We are always surprised if those faculty members even have jobs next term. This is a death sentence in online teaching. Claiming academic freedom will get you only so far! All in all, be responsive to your managers and your students, even if only to say that you'll be responding to a request "Thursday morning." Follow through with that commitment, which will require scheduling and organization on your part.

Getting Organized

Getting, being, and staying organized are critical factors for successfully managing your bosses and their requests, keeping everyone happy, and making your mark in your online teaching career. You may choose to use a technological method of organization, as discussed in the technology chapter (Chapter 10), or you may choose to use the more traditional approach of sticky notes and agenda books. Either way, record even the most mundane things, unless you have the memory of a superhero. Whatever your approaches to scheduling and to life in general, find something that works for you and stick with it.

Additional Work Opportunities within the Schools You Work For

Once you have a job at a university, you will want to expand your workload if you like working for it (or reduce it if not). After you have an established positive rapport with management, you can look for additional opportunities within the school you work for. Sometimes the best way to do this is to simply send an e-mail to your boss indicating that you enjoy working for XYZ School. Indicate why your schedule has opened (you dropped some schools you don't feel have credible programs, for instance) and then explain that you are pursuing further opportunities at schools you enjoy and with managers you respect (use your own words here; this needs to reflect your true thoughts and feelings). Then simply ask for additional opportunities. You may suggest course revision, development work, or even courses you saw on the schedule of classes that you feel qualified to teach and are interested in. Either way, your candor will prove effective in showing your interest and also perhaps finding additional opportunities. You may ask your boss what that university requires of someone to be a subject matter expert, and then clearly state what you're an expert in.

Some areas in which you may be able to pick up additional work include new course development, minor and major course revision, book evaluation, or additional courses in the same or new programs, as well as becoming a lead faculty member, dissertation committee member, comprehensive exam committee member, committee chair, or mentor. You may also pick up an additional workload at residencies or school colloquia, which are usually required for doctoral and some master's learners.

You may be asked to serve as a quality auditor for new faculty, wherein you evaluate how well a new instructor is meeting the school standards in delivering a course. You may also be asked to serve as a quality coach and spend several weeks working one-on-one with an instructor who failed his/her quality audit. As you might surmise, if you are asked to be either a quality coach or a quality auditor, it is indeed a compliment; it means they see you as a role model, and you should take these jobs when offered. If nothing else, you know that you are not being audited if you are on the auditing team!

Lessons Learned

We didn't want to end the book without offering up some of our own personal lessons learned. With more than 20 years of combined experience, we make these suggestions so you will listen to the voice in your head that may speak to you on occasion about various situations.

So let us begin with some thoughts on ethics. First, you will figure out sooner or later who you want to work for in part based on their ethics policies (or lack thereof). Go with your gut; if you don't feel right about something, you can easily test the waters by standing up for what you believe is right and seeing how administration reacts. An unfavorable reaction (one that doesn't meet your ethical standards) is, in our opinion, a good reason to leave.

Keep yourself well networked in the online world. You will be amazed at who will show up in a training class that you already know, or who will be made a dean at a college you work at. Likewise, you never know who from your doctoral committee you might end up working *with* as peers later! Don't burn bridges. Make your reasons for doing things clear.

Read documentation that the university sends out. As cumbersome as it might be sometimes, particularly if you work with students in a doctoral setting, understanding what you're doing and why will keep you out of hot water and make you look good to those who count.

Don't spread yourself too thin when you're teaching and mentoring. Even though more contracts mean more pay, and it is tempting to take on all you can, be choosy when you have the opportunity to be. If it appears that you are not good at anything, you will soon find yourself with nothing.

Get contracts in place for work up front. If you teach a class, you should have a contract before the course begins, but you will sometimes find that a contract won't come your way until the course has already begun. be sure to keep a copy for your files and let the university know if you haven't been paid. You may also be asked to develop a course; it isn't unusual that you might ask for right of first refusal in teaching it. You should also know exactly how much you are being paid and what the conditions of the contract are. Make sure that you keep universities honest, keep track of your contracts, and demand that universities honor them. In the online world, administration seems to change so frequently that sometimes promises are left unfulfilled. This is unacceptable, and any administrator who doesn't make good on promises needs to pay up. Be fair, but be firm. You are expected to honor your contract as a faculty member, and they should be expected to honor theirs as administrators.

Have a backup plan for light teaching loads. Sometimes during the summer enrollment drops. Every time this occurs, your paycheck drops with it. This might be an opportunity for a mini-vacation. You might want to consult or do paid research on the side for extra income, particularly in these situations. When you don't have classes, remember to remind your bosses that you do in fact exist and are eager to work hard for them.

Don't ever try to fake it. If you don't know a subject, don't teach it. Sometimes universities are so pressed to find faculty that they may offer you a contract for a course you aren't qualified to teach. If you accept such a contract, you will be doing your students a disservice and you will look foolish, not to mention that it is highly unethical. If you are a quick study and know the topic relatively well, then use your own moral compass as a guide.

Don't accept courses to teach and then subcontract the actual work to family and friends. While this sounds enterprising, *you* were hired as the faculty member, and it is highly unethical to have someone else interact with your students while pretending to be you. You are certainly free to ask for help from your colleagues with regard to specific course issues or get a second opinion on a grade, but you are ultimately responsible for what is posted in the course room and will be held accountable. If you truly need someone to substitute for you (because of a personal emergency or vacation), be up-front with your boss and you will probably find him or her to be very understanding and supportive; be willing to cover for someone else, too, when their needs arise.

Ignore the petty battles that occur in some faculty newsletters. Getting involved makes you look like a whiner. If something important is of interest, perhaps a quick note to your boss stating, "I noticed in the faculty e-mail list that X was being discussed. I had a thought on how we might solve that issue, as I've noticed it, too. I recommend [fill in with your ideas]."

Don't lower standards for your students just to gain popularity points. Education is precious, and for some reason it seems to be the only commodity in which customers want less than what they paid for. If you spell out your standards to your students on day one, you can hold them to these standards without fear. During the last week of a course, don't be surprised to see several of your students with family emergencies, some of which are obviously fabricated; it becomes impossible to decipher the real excuses from the made-up ones, so the best advice is to stick to your stated policies unless the student provides documentation of the excuse or you are directed by your boss to make an exception. If you find yourself being questioned for failing students who deserve to fail and lectured on how the school is a business first and cannot afford to lose these students (or their money), then you have found yourself in the midst of a diploma mill wanna-be. It may be accredited and legal, but is willing to sacrifice academic standards for the sake of money; if this makes you cringe, then leave. Remember that there are many places to teach and you don't need to sell your soul for this lifestyle.

Adding Opportunities at New Universities

Having experience as an adjunct at various schools, even at some of the less-than-prestigious colleges, will help you find jobs elsewhere and will open doors to other positions. If you have a master's degree, you should seriously consider working on a doctorate. If you are already a doctor, consider improving your professional skills, attending seminars regularly, and reading and taking courses on being a more effective teacher. When you complete something of significance, send an e-mail to your boss to update your profile.

218

One way to add new universities is to network with people in your training course. Be careful not to e-mail your training facilitators! Adjuncts often discuss what happens at other schools that they work for in a different school's training session. This is done to find best practices, share personal examples, and so forth. If you notice Joe Smith works for XYZ College and you'd like to work there, perhaps send him an e-mail introducing yourself and asking him how he applied and began working for XYZ. You might want to have some online conversations in the discussion boards first to make your name more familiar to Joe before you send a message. It's important to offer something in return! If someone refers you to a university, offer to do the same. Once you make online friends and contacts, you should create a list of people you send new opportunities or referrals to regularly, and ask that they do the same for you. You will find an incredibly networked environment in the online teaching world. Some people are better at networking than others, but in an online environment you need to do it and you need to do it well. You will quickly make friends (and possibly enemies), so be careful what you say. Chances are the person you offend knows someone or works for someone where you work or where you apply. Remember, a bad referral has your name written all over it!

It isn't unusual or unexpected to work for and inquire at many universities at the same time. You may choose to list only some of them on your resume once you work for many, but that's okay also. Just be sure you can manage your workload effectively.

Managing Your Cash Flow: The Ups and Downs of Contract Work

So you're an adjunct and you're working online, and life is good. But you'll find very quickly that you have a rather peculiar cash flow situation; for some months, you will have none! Every school has its own pay schedule. Some are monthly, some biweekly, some quarterly—you name it.

You will need to budget yourself well, and find a way to keep track of which schools owe you and what they owe you for, as well as when the amount was payable to you and when you should receive it. If you aren't paid within a week or so of the expected time frame, send a tactful e-mail to your boss and/or the administrative assistant inquiring after the status. In other words, don't count on being paid promptly, and do assume you will need to be your own accountant. Many schools aren't good at tracking adjunct pay—in particular, the items that you may be paid hourly or all at once for.

For instance, one time Dr. Babb was asked to modify a course, and when she was finished, her boss indicated he'd be cutting her pay in half for budgetary reasons. Although initially she was quite angry about this, she decided to let it go because this particular university regularly offered her lead positions that paid relatively well. She got to travel and speak a lot, and truly enjoyed working for her boss and the university. She also strongly believed in its mission, so it wasn't worth complaining about a few hundred dollars.

In essence, don't count on anything by any particular date, unless a university has a decent payroll system. Some schools send out a pay schedule in advance, and even send you a new one when your course load is modified. These are great schools and they often pay every two weeks, leaving you less stressed.

Some universities will make you a W-2 contractor, meaning they will withhold taxes. Other schools will send you a 1099 form for your work at the end of the year as an independent contractor. We have set up businesses to manage our money and maximize our work-related expenses to be deductible for income tax purposes. Talk with a tax professional and/or accountant if you aren't sure how to do this and you're beginning to make money teaching. The fee won't be worth it for income of $10,000 per year, but when you start making six figures and the tax man comes to collect his 30 percent, you won't be a happy camper if you haven't planned properly. It isn't unusual to have many W-2s and 1099s at the end of the year; at the end of the year 2005 Dr. Babb collected 14 1099s and 7 W-2s, which made her accountant cringe!

You'll need to find a way to track your income and what is outstanding. There are two simple ways we recommend you do this. Spreadsheets are easy, but the expense tracking and tax capabilities of QuickBooks are a bit more robust. You may decide to track what you are owed with a simple spreadsheet with two tabs, "paid" and "to be paid." Table 11.1 shows an example of a spreadsheet for tracking income.

As you can see, there are several things you'll need to track besides courses that you teach: residency money (attending or presenting at a residency), independent study or individual learners at schools that pay per student, expense reports for various activities, dissertation or comprehensive exam committees, course development, and course revisions. You name it, and you need to track it. Once things get more complicated, your spreadsheet will grow, but it will also enable you to add a little predictability to your income (lack of predictability is one of the tough aspects of teaching online).

Table 11.1 **Income–Tracking Spreadsheet**

School	Contract	Amount	Billed	Paid	Due Date
XYZ	Course Development 8101	$3,000.00	$3,000.00	—	6-15-07
ABC	Expense Report, Faculty Workshop	$1,050.00	$1,050.00	$700, waiting for second check	6-1-07
123	Student B, Independent Study	$ 150.00	$ 150.00	—	6-15-07

QuickBooks or programs like it will let you create a business and then track expenses and accounts payable (AP). You'd essentially enter your items into an AP system that will print reports and show you what is owed and when it was due. From this system you can also create invoices, which some schools will want you to do. You are, after all, running a business as an independent contractor. You might be signing HR documents, but you are still your own business manager. Talk with your tax professional about the benefits of using such software.

In general, it's a good idea to obtain the advice of a tax expert. There are various ways you can set up your business for a high workload, and there are various tasks you'll need to do for each setup, like possibly having an Employer Identification Number registered with the Internal Revenue Service (IRS), for instance, so you need to talk with a professional or look the task up online and do it yourself. By incorporating yourself or creating a sole proprietorship, you open yourself up to incredible tax advantages along with some unexpected costs. Most of the time it is worthwhile to either incorporate or create some other sort of an official business.

Also, be sure to check on the requirements of your county or city for business licenses. Some cities require that if you do business at all out of your home, you have to have a business license. This is a way for the city to generate revenue. Some states' franchise tax boards and state tax authorities report your business activity to the city, and you'll receive a lovely letter requiring you to register your business. You don't want to be scrambling, so find out the rules ahead of time.

Not All Teaching Opportunities Are Created Equal

By now you have a good feel for what will take tremendous time with little financial gain, what will take time with a great feel-good factor, and what isn't worth doing, plain and simple. If you can find a way to quantify your time and to document what is most worth your effort, you can give good (positively spun) feedback to your bosses and also make decisions later when your workload is high and you need to weed out the bad stuff—or, if you're lucky, the not so hot stuff. Start noting which universities require more of your free time and don't pay for substantial efforts of work. These may be on your hit list when you have one.

Referring Others

Once you're in a university and you've earned respect (you may even be a subject matter expert), it's perfectly acceptable (and universities appreciate it) if you refer qualified candidates. "Qualified" doesn't necessarily mean they are your friends! They might also be your friends, but they must be people you're willing to put your reputation on the line for. If you're highly respected at a university, your selected candidates may skip through much of the interview process. You may have been hired at some schools this way. As we've said before, networking is very strong and an intense requirement in this online world. Screen your referrals as you would if you were doing the hiring. One mistake can damage your reputation, and it isn't worth it. Dr. Babb has exactly three people she'd refer for online positions at institutions where she teaches—three, that's it. How many have asked? Probably hundreds. Dr. Mirabella has about 10 people he'd actively refer to institutions where he teaches, but would willingly serve as a reference for a rare few of his select mentees looking to break into teaching at schools where he doesn't teach (figuring they have proven themselves to him through a difficult dissertation process). Likewise, hundreds have asked him for referrals over the years.

Remember to be kind to those who help you, as it is only fair. If you are not comfortable actively referring a person, you can still direct that person to the web site, as there is a difference between giving directions for getting hired and personally sending in someone's resume with a recommendation for hiring.

Go For It!

Working as an adjunct will give you tremendous flexibility to do all sorts of things, like write books, for instance! Remember that there are many ways to boost your career, and try not to look at your newfound free time as vacation time. You need to publish, you need to research, and you need to put yourself out there to truly make it in a market that is going to get competitive quickly. Make yourself invaluable to students and to your bosses; this will only appreciate your value to universities and add to your influence. The better networked you are and the more you are liked, the more doors will open. Stay focused; stay tuned into yourself, your managers, and, more important, your students. As more people realize what a lucrative and terrific career this is, expect the supply and demand to rise (we hope demand rises more than supply!).

Above all else, have fun. A Chinese proverb says, "There are two kinds of jobs a man can do—the one he loves and the one he does best. If they're both the same, he's truly blessed." If you're not good at teaching, don't enjoy it, or don't ever see yourself liking the profession, then stop. If you are not having fun at a particular school, try something different or just quit that school. Every school is different, and every course is different. Each of you will not fit into every school. Some experiences will be a joy and some will be painful, sometimes due to the particular set of students you have, sometimes due to the nature of the course, sometimes due to your boss or school politics, and sometimes due to things going on in your personal life. Just remember to do what you love and love what you do. Make a good living and have a great life.

Best of luck!

Should you have questions or comments for the authors, suggestions for future material, or tips, feel free to e-mail us at dani@teachonlinebook .com or jim@teachonlinebook.com, or visit our web site at www.teach onlinebook.com. We offer numerous community forums, places to share job search tips, information on job openings, and advice from the authors! We offer seminars, supplemental material, and newsletters on our web site, too!

Sources

Good teaching is one-fourth preparation and three-fourths pure theater.

—Gail Godwin

AdAware (www.adaware.com). Software available for download at www.download.com.

Bartlett, Thomas, and Scott Smallwood. "Psst. Wanna Buy a Ph.D.?" and "What's a Diploma Mill?" Special Report. Chronicle of Higher Education 50, issue 42 (June 25, 2004): 9. Retrieved from the Internet at www.chronicle.com.

Blackboard.com. Retrieved from the Internet on January 28, 2006, at www.blackboard.com/company/.

Capriccioso, Rob. "Help Wanted: Low-Cost Adjuncts. InsideHigherEd.com (October 31, 2005). www.insidehighered.com/news/2005/10/31/adjunct.

Chronicle of Higher Education. "More Faculty Jobs Go to Part-Timers." Chronicle of Higher Education 51, issue 39, p. A8. Retrieved from the Internet at www.chronicle.com.

Sources

Coates, T. "Concerning Social Software, Mass-Amateurisation, Design and Future Media: What You Should Know Before Starting a Doctorate." (2004). Retrieved from www.plasticbag.org/archives/2004/07/what_you_should_know_before_starting_a_doctorate.shtml on March 17, 2006.

CUPA. Survey. Retrieved from www.cupahr.org.

DeVry Online. "Requirements for Online Teachers." Retrieved from the Internet February 2006 at www.devry.edu/whydevry/online_options_technical_specs.jsp.

Dill, D., and L. Morrison. "EdD and PhD Research Training in the Field of Higher Education: A Survey and a Proposal." Review of Higher Education 8, no. 2 (1985): 169–186.

Download.com at. www.download.com.

eCollege. Retrieved from the Internet on January 28, 2006, at www.ecollege.com/company/About.learn.

eFax.com. Software available for download at www.efax.com.

Gmail from Google. E-mail accounts available at www.gmail.com.

Hotmail. E-mail accounts available at www.hotmail.com.

HP iPAQ Windows CE PDA at www.hp.com (2006).

Indiana Wesleyan University (www.indwes.edu).

InsideHigherEd.com. "Moving Beyond Tenure." Confessions of a Community College Dean." Written by "Dean Dad" online at www.insidehighered.com/views/2006/02/21/ccdean (2006).

Knight, R. "Number of Doctorates Awarded in U.S. Rises." FinancialTimes.com (November 30, 2005).

K7.net. Software available for download at www.k7.net.

Liberty University (www.liberty.edu).

McAfee. Software available for download at www.mcafee.com.

Microsoft (www.microsoft.com).

Murdock, P. "Fast Tech: 2005 Winners and Losers." Forbes: Stock Focus. Retrieved from the Internet on January 27, 2006, at www.forbes.com/2006/01/26/lifecell-celgene-winnerslosers-cz_pm_0127sf.html?partner=yahootix.

Sources

MyFax.com. Software available for download at www.myfax.com

National Science Foundation. "Science & Engineering Doctorates: 2004." Retrieved from the Internet at www.nsf.gov/statistics/nsf06308/tables.htm.

New Mexico State University. "Detail and Characteristics of a Doctor of Education vs. a Doctor of Philosophy." Retrieved from the Internet at http://education.nmsu.edu/emd/studentResources/EdD%20vs%20PhD.pdf (2005).

Nixon, Thomas. "Avoid College Degree Scams." AdultEd/Continuing Education at About, Inc. Retrieved from the Internet at http://adulted.about.com (2006).

Norton AntiVirus. Software available for download at www.norton.com.

Olmscheid, A. Capella University Career Center personal interview (2006).

Palm (www.palmone.com).

Phillips, V. "Are Online Degrees Really as Good as Their Campus Counterparts?" GetEducated.com. Retrieved from the Internet at www.geteducated.com (2005).

PR NewsWire, FireCall. "Blackboard Inc. Recognized by the Red Herring Small Cap 100." Retrieved from the Internet on December 12, 2005, at http://biz.yahoo.com/prnews/051212/dcm015.html?.v=29.

Puzziferro, Maria, Director of Continuing Education at Colorado State University, Denver Campus, personal interview conducted February 2006.

Schnitzer, M., and Crosby, L.S. "Recruitment and Development of Online Adjunct Instructors." (2003). Retrieved from the Internet at www.westga.edu/~distance/ojdla/summer62/crosby_schnitzer62.html.

Skype. Software available for download at www.skype.com.

Sloan Consortium. "Growing by Degrees: Online Education in the United States." (2005).

Smallwood, S. "Doctor Dropout." Chronicle of Higher Education. (January 16, 2004). Retrieved from the Internet at www.chronicle.com.

Smith, S. "NewsLook." Software for nNewsgroups available for download at www.ghytred.com/NewsLook (2006).

Sources

SpyBot Search and Destroy. Software available for download at www
.downloads.com.

U.S. Census Bureau population statistics at www.census.gov/.

U.S. Department of Education. "Financial Aid for Postsecondary Students." Retrieved from the Internet at www.ed.gov/admins/finaid/
accred/accreditation.html.

WebCT. Retrieved from the Internet on January 28, 2006, at www
.webct.com.

Wilson, Shari. "The Transient Academic." *The Nomad Scholar.* Inside
HigherEd.com (February 17, 2006).

WorldWideLearn. "Online High School Diploma Programs & Courses." Retrieved from the Internet at www.worldwidelearn.com/online-degrees/
online-high-school-courses.htm.

Index

AACSB. *See* Association to Advance Collegiate Schools of Business (AACSB)
ABD. *See* "All but dissertation" (ABD)
Academia, online education and, 17
Accreditation mills, 26
Accredited online schools, 22–23, 24
Adjunct faculty. *See also* Online adjunct faculty
  building career as, 24
  compensation of, 58, 146–147
  earning pay, 31
  finding link for applying as, 78
  health care and, 48
  job security of, 33
  jobs in higher education, 32
  as online teaching position, 52
  opportunities for, 21, 30–31
  reading university documentation, 216
  requirements of, 61–64, 124–127
  schools' need for, 49–51
  types of applicants for, 29
  unionizing of, 32
  upsides and downsides to life of, 57–61
  working in different schools, 66
Adjunct Nation, 76
AIU Online. *See* American InterContinental University Online (AIU Online)

"All but dissertation" (ABD), 46
American InterContinental University Online (AIU Online), 41, 49
Antispam, 198–199
Antispy software, 201
Apex Learning, 55
Assignments, adjunct faculty and, 63
Association to Advance Collegiate Schools of Business (AACSB), 23
Asynchronous online courses, 62, 67
Attendance tracking, workload and, 169
Auditory learning style, 18
Auto-generated response:
  as acknowledgment to job application, 136–137
  as rejection to job application, 135–136
Axia College, 63, 163

Bachelor's degrees, online teaching opportunities with, 10–11, 53
Backup hard drives, 202
Backups:
  plan for light teaching loads, 217
  teaching online and, 187–189
Baker College, 41, 61
Balancing time, in online teaching jobs, 65–66

Index

235

Index

Nontraditional program, pursuing for master's degree, 39
Nontraditional universities, 24–25, 54, 119–121
North Central Association of Schools and Colleges (NCA), 22
Northcentral University, 25, 38, 41, 52
Northwest Association of Schools and Colleges (NWCCU), 22
Not-for-profit traditional universities, 23–24
Not on Your Life U situation, 175–176
NWCCU. *See* Northwest Association of Schools and Colleges (NWCCU)

Office hours, adjunct faculty and, 62–63
Office suites, 201
Ofstedal, Julie, 92
Olmscheid, Amy, 92
On-ground universities, 157
Online adjunct faculty. *See also* Adjunct faculty
  asynchronous online courses and, 62
  attending events, 73
  balancing work and home, 180–181
  Blackboard and, 159–160, 164
  communication and, 176–178
  demand and supply for, 48
  doing what your are good at, 178–179
  eCollege and, 162–163, 165–166
  first impression as, 130
  Great to Work for You U situation, 174–175
  I Can Live with You U situation, 175
  jobs in higher education, 32
  meetings, online universities and, 62
  newsgroups and, 166–167
  Not on Your Life U situation, 175–176
  opportunities for, 21
  pay rates and development of, 70–71
  pay vs. workload, 167–174
  pros and cons of tools used by, 163–167
  teaching workshops, 74

using e-mail, 179
WebCT and, 160–161, 165
working as, overview of, 157–159
Online courses. *See also* Online education
  auditory learning style and, 18
  colleges offering, 23–25
  e-mail for, 64
  kinesthetic learning style and, 18
  learners and, 1
  payment for, 72
  pay negotiation for, 70
  pursuing traditional university for, 38
  synchronous and asynchronous, 62
  visual learning style and, 17–18
Online degrees. *See also* Online courses
  hiring faculty with, 21, 39
  legitimacy of, in corporate America, 20–21
Online education:
  nontraditional and bitraditional universities and, 24–25
  option of, 20
  phenomenon of, 16
  reality of, 16–17
Online high schools, teaching positions in, 55–56
Online managers, using ping with, 210
Online organizations, 157
Online programs, as step in getting master's degree, 37–40
Online schools. *See also* Online education
  accreditation of, 22–23
  adjunct faculty and, 30–33
  colleges offering online courses, 23–25
  degree legitimacy in corporate America, 20–21
  diploma mills and scams, 25–27
  finding, 37
  interview processes of, 116–124
  learning college material in, 17–18
  opportunity for online faculty, 21
  reality of online education, 16–17

236

Index

Professionals, online teaching and, 11–12

Published author, as quality of adjunct faculty, 125

"Publish or perish" mentality, 54

Puzziferro, Maria, 29, 127–128

Quality of Service (QoS), 191

Questionnaire, interview, 117

Referrals, 223–224

Regional accrediting bodies, 22

Relationship maintenance, in virtual world, 209–211

Requirements:
 of deans for adjunct faculty, 124–127
 for online teaching positions, 53–55
 of responsiveness, 64

Responsiveness:
 proving, 134–140
 as quality of adjunct faculty, 64, 125, 129
 students' needs, 213–214
 training and, 149

Resume:
 curriculum vitae and, 90–93
 samples of, 93–111

Retired individuals, online teaching opportunities and, 12–13, 29

SACS. *See* Southern Association of Colleges and Schools (SACS)

Salaries. *See* Compensation

Scams, 25–27

Scanners, 195–196

Scholar-practitioner approach, 43

School ethics, 173

School requirements, teaching online technology and, 203–204

Schools. *See also* Online schools
 finding programs in, 77
 with highest enrollments, 40–42
 locating, for first job, 75–77
 pay rates at, 70

SearchNetworking.com, 210

Self-directed learner mentoring, workload and, 169

Setting flexible system, 205

Skills for teaching online courses, 19

Skype, 191

Sloan Consortium report, 2005, 16–17

Smith, Simon, software of, 190

Software and keys, 202–203

Southern Association of Colleges and Schools (SACS), 22

Statement of teaching philosophy, 111–112

Stay-at-home parents, online teaching and, 12

Staying in touch, 213

Strengths:
 addressing in interviews, 129–134
 online teaching jobs and, 67

Student(s):
 adjunct faculty payment per, 72
 popularity with and not lowering teaching standards, 218

Subcontracts, 217

Subject, teaching and knowledge of, 217

Subject line, in introductory message, 81

Subject matter expert (SME), 71, 132

Synchronous online courses, 62, 67

Teachers, traditional, teaching online, 29

Teaching experience:
 online teaching jobs and, 47–49
 as quality for adjunct faculty, 124

Teaching online. *See* Online teaching

Teaching opportunities:
 graduate degrees and, 36–40, 42–46
 growing business and, 222–223
 for online faculty, 21
 recommendations for, 35–36
 schools with highest enrollment and, 40–42

Index